Amish Quilts
of Lancaster County

Patricia T. Herr

**The Esprit Quilt Collection of the Heritage
Center Museum, Lancaster, Pennsylvania**

Schiffer Publishing Ltd

4880 Lower Valley Road, Atglen, PA 19310 USA

Dedication

To all the people who have contributed to this effort of bringing the Amish quilts home to Lancaster County, and in memory of Louise Stoltzfus for her support and strong personal and scholarly interest.

Library of Congress Cataloging-in-Publication Data
Herr, Patricia T., 1936-
Amish quilts of Lancaster County / by Patricia T. Herr.
p. cm.
ISBN 0-7643-2017-3 (pbk.)
1. Quilts, Amish--Pennsylvania--Lancaster County. I. Title.
NK9112 .H467 2004
746.46'088'289774815--dc22
2003024667

Designed by Bonnie M. Hensley
Cover design by Bruce Waters
Type set in Fontleroy Brown/Aldine 721 BT

ISBN: 0-7643-2017-3
Printed in China

Published by Schiffer Publishing Ltd.
4880 Lower Valley Road
Atglen, PA 19310
Phone: (610) 593-1777; Fax: (610) 593-2002
E-mail: Info@schifferbooks.com
For the largest selection of fine reference books on this and related subjects,
please visit our web site catalog at **www.schifferbooks.com**
We are always looking for people to write books on new and related subjects.
If you have an idea for a book, please contact us at the above address.

This book may be purchased from the publisher.
Include $3.95 for shipping. Please try your bookstore first. You may write for a free catalog.

In Europe, Schiffer books are distributed by
Bushwood Books
6 Marksbury Ave. Kew Gardens
Surrey TW9 4JF England
Phone: 44 (0)20 8392-8585; Fax: 44 (0)20 8392-9876
E-mail: info@bushwoodbooks.co.uk
Free postage in the UK. Europe: air mail at cost.
Please try your bookstore first.

Contents

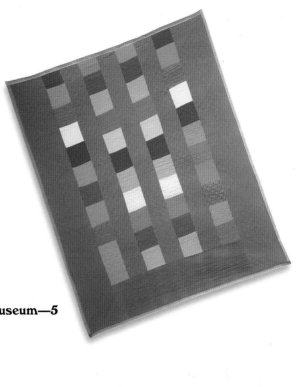

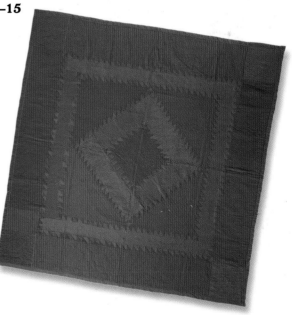

Acknowledgments

Many people have helped with this Lancaster Amish quilt project. When it was an impossible dream, a committee that I choose to call "The Fabulous Four"—Donna Albert, quilt designer; Cindy Hampton, specialist in economic development; Julie McCollough, fiber artist; and the late Louise Stoltzfus, Amish quilt historian—attempted to convince me that we had to bring these quilts home. The improbable idea was presented to Peter Seibert, president of the Heritage Center Museum, who thought it worthy of consideration. Late-night calls and early-morning meetings with Carrie Nunan and Jack Buckwalter helped the idea evolve into a possibility. Early financial support from several foundations and the backing of the Board of Trustees of the Heritage Center Museum of Lancaster County made the impossible dream develop into a viable option. The hard work of the museum staff and trustees and the continued support of our many friends and donors made this dream a reality.

Once the Heritage Center Museum had the Esprit quilts in hand, we literally could spread out our work before us. With the help of Rachel and Kenny Pellman we looked at this collection and the manuscript from many different viewpoints. It is a significant repository and design source for modern artists, folk art collectors, students of American history and folklore, fiber arts specialists, quilt designers and makers, and textilians throughout the world. With Rachel's assistance each quilt was carefully examined and measured, and notes and photographs were recorded for future in-depth study and the production of this book. Quilt designers and makers can thank Rachel for the practical information included. We hope this will lead our readers to experiment and use the material in many imaginative ways.

Many people lent their valuable assistance to this effort as work progressed. Julie Silber, former curator of the Esprit collection and a principal in the Quilt Complex, Albion, California, has continued to be supportive and helpful in every way. Eugene Moore spent many hours using his fine editorial skills. Bruce Waters kindly provided exquisite scenes he had photographed of Amish farms and families and more photographs were cheerfully provided by Jessica Abernathy, Public Relations Manager of the Lancaster County Pennsylvania Dutch Convention & Visitors Bureau.

I would like to thank these generous donors who, by giving funds for the purchase of the quilt collection, have made this all possible:

Stakeholder
Oxford Foundation
Richard Von Hess Foundation
Irene N. Walsh

Sunshine & Shadows Supporter
Dr. & Mrs. Donald M. Herr
James Frederick Steinman Foundation
James Hale Steinman Foundation

Star Supporter
Thomas A. Russo

Diamond Supporter
Ann L. & Robert K. Bowman Family Foundation
Linda L. & Patrick J. Castagna
Ellen Arnold Groff

Adopt A Quilt
Katrina L. Branting
Friend of the Heritage Center
Mrs. Linda L. Castagna
Friend of the Heritage Center
Patricia G. & Robert J. Hershock
Roger A. Herr & Anthony Sprauve
Lancaster County Foundation
Charles & Molly Milner
Jane & Paul Mueller
Willis & Elsie Shenk/WELD Foundation
Mrs. Sarah Slaymaker
Kenneth & Susan Stoudt
Paul W. & Judy S. Ware

Irish Chain
Mr. & Mrs. Dennis Cox
Mrs. Margaret Middleton Ellis
Mrs. Dorothy L. Lyet
Quilts, Inc. - Houston, Texas

Benefactor
Armstrong World Industries, Inc.
Calico Cutters Quilt Guild
Mr. Irving Budd Callman
Dr. & Mrs. Peter Christie
Abbie & Ely Gonick
Mrs. Lucinda Hampton
Dawn Heefner
Gerry & Margaret Lestz
Ms. Linda Jones McKee
The Mid-Appalachian Quilters, Inc.
John & Kate Shirk

Great Women of Lancaster
Friend of the Heritage Center
Mrs. Denise Baer
Mrs. Kendig Bare
Katrina Branting - Red Rose Quilters
Ms. Martha Bray
Mrs. Margot L. Brubaker
Ms. Rebecca S. Bumstead
Dana Chryst - The Jay Group
Dr. Alice Drum
Mrs. Judith C. Eshleman
Mrs. Karen Haley Field
Cara Keegan Fry
Mrs. Judith Farmer Fulton
Mrs. Eugene H. Gardner, Sr.
Mrs. Eugene H. Gardner, Jr.
Mary Colleen Heil
Mrs. Beth Herr
Ms. Audrey C. Hallgren
Phyllis A. Hughes
Sally & John Jarvis
Mildred H. McQueen
Red Rose Quilters Guild
Mrs. Margaret Scott
Ms. Susan K. Shearer
Margaret Thorpe - Red Rose Quilters

Marjorie A. Walker
Ms. Alethia G. White

Contributor
Ms. Susan C. Adams
Donna Albert
Betsy Amalong
Antique & Vintage Fabrid Dating Club
Rev. Dr. & Mrs. Victor Baer
Bonny Barnhill
Bayside Quilt Guild of Easton, MD
Ms. Esther H. Becker
Mr. & Mrs. George E. Becker, Jr.
Ms. Janice Beitzer
Nancy Bender
Cindy Block
Drs. Lawrence & Rita Bonchek
Sara Borr
Barbara Brackman
Judy Breen
Mrs. Sybil M. Calhoun
Ms. Lucinda R. Cawley
Ms. Pauline H. Church
Lenore M. Clarke
Rachel Cochran
Robert & Jean Cook
Bob & Kathleen DeCarli
Ms. Gail Dovalovsky
Marilyn & Bill Ebel
Faithful Circle Quilters - Columbia, MD
Andre & Carolyn Fouchet
Alice Friedrich
Friend of the Heritage Center
Mary Fritz - Red Rose Quilters
Jane D. Fry
June K. Garges
Ms. Lisa R. Garrett
Marjorie F. Gearhart
Peg Gilson

Fay Ann Grider
Mr. Timothy L. Grotzinger
Ms. Stephanie E. Hanson
Dolores J. Harnish
Ms. Dorothea C. Hartman
Patricia Hauber - Red Rose Quilters
Barbara & Scott Haverstick
Linda Henderson
Elizabeth Herr
Delores Holzwarth
Homemakers Country Quilters
Sandy Hughes
Kim Jacobs
Violette Delp Johnson
Christine Kamon
Judy Kelius
Keystone Quilters
Mrs. Marie F. Kline
Pat Flynn Kyser
Mr. & Mrs. Jay Leary
Mr. & Mrs. Ryan P. Magill
Michael & Richanne Mankey
Ms. Julie McCullough
Ms. Eleanor L. McMiname
Mrs. Lori Wilson Memmen
John & Mary Metzger
Ms. Molly Miles
Mrs. J. Alicia Miller
Stephen & Sheryl Miller
Mr. & Mrs. C. Eugene Moore
Sherry Natale
Margaret J. Neff
Mrs. Nancy S. Neff
Pat L. Nickols
Richard B. Nissley
Myrna M. Paluba
Penn Oak Quilters
Pennsylvania Quilters Assn. Inc.
PPL
Nancy Pfutzenreuter
Beverly Pierce
Julie Powell
Jean Pryzbylkowski - Red Rose Quilters
Bernice Quay
Quilt Conservancy, Columbia, MO
Ruthann Rash
Gail Richert
Josephine E. Sanders
Carla & Robert Schechner
Schoolhouse Quilter's Guild, LaVale, MD
Schoolhouse Quilter's of Salisbury, MD
Jere W. Schuler
Ms. Barbara Shand
Patricia A. Sherman
Mr. & Mrs. Steve Smoot
Marian I. Stevenson
Patricia Stone - Red Rose Quilters
Nancy N. Tanger
Phyllis R. Thompson
Ms. Cassandra Thoreson
Sally Tobias - Red Rose Quilters
Ms. Phyllis W. Twiss
Variable Star Quilters, Warrington, PA
Mr. Willem van Huystee
Laura Wakeley
Karen & Robert Weibel
Ms. Anne W. Worthington
Elizabeth Yarnall
Jean A. Zubert

Chapter 1

The Esprit Quilt Collection of the Heritage Center Museum

The story of this quilt collection began even before Doug Tompkins in San Francisco began buying examples of Lancaster Amish quilts. For most of the twentieth century quilt scholars and collectors have been actively studying quilts and publishing information about these bed coverings. The focus had always been on the makers, their techniques, the understanding of the quilts through their use within the home as decorative bed coverings, and sometimes on the historical significance of a particular quilt.

Even in the early 1900s Lancaster County drew antiques dealers and collectors from all over the East Coast. Quilts of the region have always been highly regarded by collectors and scholars. Traditionally the brightly colored and intricately worked appliquéd patterns attracted the most attention. Plain dark quilts of the Amish would occasionally appear on the auction block, but they did not attract much attention. As a result, public sales of such objects went by unnoticed.

In the late 1960s a new breed of collectors began to look at these quilts with a fresh viewpoint. Quilts were seen as art. The most notable interest seemed to be concentrated in New York City, only a short morning's drive from the farmlands of Lancaster County.

Soon collectors were asking about these bold designs that could be hung on a wall. Dealers were notifying pickers (local buyers who had close contacts with the Amish) of their interest in "those old dark wool quilts." The enthusiasm spread, prices rose, and more quilts came on the market. In 1971 a new era in quilt appreciation and collecting was punctuated by the opening of "Abstracts in American Design" at the Whitney Museum in New York City. The exhibit highlighted quilts from the collection of Jonathan Holstein and Gail van der Hoof. It was followed by the publication of Holstein's groundbreaking book *The Pieced Quilt*, which featured a Lancaster Amish Sunshine and Shadow quilt on the cover. Now these images were available not just to New York City museum visitors but also to readers around the world.

The Whitney exhibit had a far-reaching influence. Doug Tompkins, co-owner with his wife, Suzi, of Esprit de Corps Clothing of San Francisco, was a visitor to this exhibit. According to long-time Esprit curator Julie Silber,[1] Doug came home from the exhibit, assessed the bare brick walls of the Esprit corporate headquarters, and went to Julie and her partner to purchase quilts to decorate the vast open space.

For those with fashion memory, it is not hard to realize the influence these intensely deep-colored and bold-patterned Lancaster Amish quilts had on the line of Esprit clothing. Silber, who became full-time curator for the Tompkins' quilt collections, kept in touch with the most prominent and active quilt dealers of the time and gathered, advised, and assisted Tompkins with his ever-growing Amish collection. They were responsible for opening the corporate offices to the public and making the collection available for travel to museums all over the world.

When viewing the quilts in the Esprit collection, one must remember that these are not average, everyday quilts that were simply transported from Lancaster Amish homes directly to the West Coast. Silber was known in the trade as a discriminating and sophisticated buyer. Her client was looking for not just any quilt. He was not particularly interested in the cultural history of the object, the person who made it, or the techniques by which it was made. To Doug Tompkins each quilt was a work of art, and he made the final selection on this basis.

So if you were to view all of the Lancaster Amish quilts in the Esprit collection, you'd find that they do not mirror what was produced and used in the average local Amish home. They were of course selected for visual impact, condition, and personal reasons that perhaps only Doug could explain.

From this large collection of Lancaster Amish quilts amassed by Tompkins, the eighty-two Esprit quilts illustrated in this publication were carefully selected and featured in an oversized 1990 picture book with text by Robert Hughes and commentary by Julie Silber.[2] In that same year, when the Tompkinses divorced and he sold his interest in the Esprit clothing company, the Amish quilts went into storage. It was Doug's wish that this world-famous collection would continue to be seen by the public. Under the careful guidance of curator Silber, selected portions of the collection traveled throughout the United States and abroad to Japan, Australia, and Germany.

In the year 2000, when Doug Tompkins felt that he needed funds for his activities aimed at saving the rain forests in Chile, he decided to sell all of his quilts. Silber was determined to keep the group of eighty-two special quilts intact. With interest expressed by museums and auction houses throughout the country, it appeared this might not happen—that the collection might in fact be broken up. Fortunately, Silber contacted the Heritage Center Museum of Lancaster County in hopes that the quilts could "return home" to the place where they had been made.

Meanwhile this elite collection of quilts continued to draw national attention. Examples selected from the eighty-two quilts were chosen by the U. S. Postal Service to appear as a series of quilt stamps for the year 2002.

Simply to say the Heritage Center Museum purchased the collection and brought them back to Lancaster County oversimplifies the effort put forth and the plans being made for the future. The vision of the organization was to establish the Heritage Center Lancaster Quilt and Textile Museum. Efforts began promptly to make this dream a reality. The collection will always be a central part of the new museum, and portions will be available for public viewing as a part of the ongoing textile exhibits.

With the will of the Heritage Center Museum trustees and its president, Peter Seibert, the vital role of Lancaster Newspapers, Inc., the hard work of staff members, the cooperation of Julie Silber, and the generous support of so many community-minded Lancastrians and quilt lovers from around the nation, Lancaster now has the opportunity to share these special quilts with the world. They are at home in Lancaster County—where they belong!

[1]Silber's recollections are recorded in an article written by Lita Solis-Cohen in *Maine Antiques Digest*, August 2002.
[2]The book, now out of print, is titled *Amish: The Art of the Quilt* (New York: Alfred A. Knopf, 1990).

Corporate Headquarters of Esprit De Corp. Photograph taken during the 1980s when the Esprit Quilt Collection was on exhibit.

Chapter 2

Introduction to the Amish Culture

Kenneth and Rachel Pellman

Amish quilts have captured attention and imagination in corners of the world far distant from their origins. Prestigious urban museums exhibit Amish quilts to vast numbers of visitors. Multinational corporate offices adorn their walls with quilts from the Amish. International art and antique collectors dress their digs with quilts from the hands of Amish quilters. Far beyond regional colloquialism or national limits, Amish quilts garner worldwide appeal for their quiet, bold, and simple design. Both the modern eye and traditional spirit welcome their strong charisma and their daring juxtapositions of design and color.

Amish quilts can be admired on a variety of levels. But with a bit of background into the people from whom these treasures have come, one's appreciation can deepen for these gems from yesteryear.

Amish origins

Amish origins are traced to the sixteenth-century Protestant Reformation. In those days, the church and state were closely linked. Newborns became citizens of the state and were baptized as infants, making them members of the Catholic Church. Reformer Martin Luther and some of his contemporaries sought more separation between those two institutions. An impatient left-wing contingent of the Reformation agreed with Luther's basic premise but were led to take the movement further, creating a third choice that was neither completely Protestant nor Catholic. This radical group gave new authority to the scriptures and considered the New Testament a literal guide for life. Their interpretation differed from the mores of the existent church and state. These reformers considered Jesus' life on earth to be a model for correct living. They believed that people could truly be disciples of Jesus in contemporary society by following his teachings and life example. Daily discipleship was a way of life. But this effort at faithful living was neither popular nor readily received by the status quo. These activists were not a quiet group. Convinced of their correct Biblical interpretation, they publicly and aggressively identified and challenged many established but, in their opinions, lax and unethical practices of Catholics, Protestants and governmental officials. Several major issues separated this third alternative from the existent church: 1) the practice of adult voluntary (instead of infant) baptism, 2) complete separation of church and state, and 3) an ethic of peace, nonviolence as a way of life, and refusal to swear oaths.

The first of these peculiar practices views baptism as a symbol of personal commitment and alignment with the life and teachings of Jesus. A literal following of Jesus' words and example may be neither accepted nor tolerated by the majority of society. Infants could not comprehend the gravity of that decision. Agreement to a way of life with those potential ramifications should be undertaken only voluntarily by adults. Practicing adult baptism earned these reformers the nickname Anabaptists, meaning re-baptizers. This arrant group baptized its first adult members in Switzerland on January 21, 1525. Enduring a long history of martyrdom and persecution by Protestants, Catholics and the state, this movement grew and flourished throughout Europe. It spread quickly north to Germany, the Netherlands, and many regions of Western Europe. Relentless attempts by the church and state officials failed to eradicate this bothersome bunch. In the remainder of the sixteenth century, thousands of Anabaptists were killed in gruesome and heinous ways.

Separation of church and state resulted in rank ordering of these two entities for the Anabaptists. They were willing to follow state decrees and laws until and unless they conflicted with their understandings of faithful discipleship to Jesus. Church and state operate with different rules and mandates. When in conflict, Anabaptist allegiance went to the church and away from government.

Moving peace and nonviolence from a concept to a way of life translated into refusal to bear arms. They would not use violent means to defend their country nor use force to protect themselves when persecuted by church and state officials. (*The Martyr's Mirror*, a 1,200-page tome first published in 1660, chronicles the events in this period of Anabaptist history. The book, still in print, is in many Amish homes today. It reminds them of their differences with the larger world and helps keep their resolve keen in the effort to live as faithful disciples of Jesus.)

In Friesland, an articulate and prolific Dutch Catholic priest, Menno Simons, joined the Anabaptist movement. Menno was an influential preacher, and the group was eventually nicknamed Mennonites. Zealous efforts to remain faithful resulted in internal bickering. Differing opinions, domineering personalities, and varying points of view could not retain group cohesion. Acculturation was becoming more common within the ranks of the faithful, and some of the strict separation issues were more relaxed. Internal struggle split the group in 1693. Led by Swiss-born Jakob Ammann, this faction became known as Amish. Ammann, concerned that the Anabaptists had wandered too far from the original convictions that separated them from the mainline Protestant Reformation, introduced more tangible rules to determine the group parameters. This new group started in Alsace and spread northward through the Rhine Valley of current-day France and Germany.

The ongoing search for religious freedom brought Amish to North America in two major migrations – the first in the mid-1700s, the latter in the early 1800s. Arriving in the east, many settled initially in southeastern Pennsylvania. The search for new frontiers enticed some families to push westward. Large Amish communities remain in Pennsylvania, Ohio, and Indiana, but settlements are also located in more than two dozen other states and in Ontario, Canada. There are no Old Order Amish communities in Europe.

Many Amish people look to history as they seek to live godly lives in contemporary society. It helps interpret the present and anticipate the future.

They are a Christian group, and their life directives come from the Bible, which they believe is God's word to the world. Amish interpretations of the Biblical story are understood through the sieve of the historical and current church. The church community weighs and assesses the calls of God and through that joint process, determines the practices conducive to faithful living.

The Amish are a live and vibrant group whose membership has doubled in the last two decades. Change happens slowly and deliberately as they consider the past and anticipate the future.

Amish Today

Information about the people and quilts displayed in this book represent the Old Order Amish community of Lancaster County, in southeastern Pennsylvania. This is the oldest Amish settlement in North America.

Conformity

In order to maintain group norms and community conformity, the Amish draw clear boundaries for day-to-day living. These lines include strict stipulations and clear understandings on transportation, dress, education, the use of technology, and daily life choices. As one looks in from the outside, the mandates can appear restrictive and confining, limiting options for group members. From the inside looking out, the perspective is different. For most Amish persons, aligning oneself with the group provides freedom to live and work within a community that is supportive, encouraging, and fulfilling.

Deciding to join the church commonly happens between eighteen and twenty-one years of age. Amish teenagers, like many others, test boundaries and assert their independence. Some break the rules, step over the lines, and disappoint their church and family. However, after "sowing wild oats," most Amish youth join the church becoming committed life-long members. Their rural background may make them timid of more culturally diverse urban centers. The choice to stop formal education after Grade Eight eliminates many vocational choices. But many are bright, well-informed persons who, having considered other possibilities, choose to be Amish.

Amish children appear to be miniatures of their parents. They dress, live, travel, and go to church following the example of the adults around them. It is not unusual for children to grow up with parents and grandparents sharing the same homestead. Grandparents often live in a "dawdy" (grandparent) house, an independent but attached addition to the larger house. Though they live separately, there is great opportunity for interaction between generations.

Children are born and received into the family as a gift from God. Growing up and growing old occur within the embrace of the family. When death approaches, it is viewed as a part of the natural order and a return to God. Untimely death, though difficult and heart-breaking, is also viewed as a part of God's plan and beyond human understanding. There is comfort in community and the belief that God is in control.

Dress

Dress is a powerful tool in establishing group identity. The church determines modes of dress for both men and women. Most Amish clothing is made at home. Women wear modestly styled dresses constructed of solid-colored fabrics. Young girls wear a range of colors including blues, purples, greens, dark reds, and pinks. Older women wear a more limited palate of subdued shades with a black cape and apron covering a large part of the dress. Young girls may have snaps or buttons on dresses. Older girls and women use straight pins for dress closures. Very young girls are not required to wear head coverings (except to church), but older girls and women wear an organdy cap or "covering" whenever they appear in public. Hair is uncut, parted in the middle, and pulled into a bun at the back of the neck. The covering fits over the back of the head and covers the bun. Kerchiefs or bandanas are often substituted for head coverings when working around the home. Amish women avoid jewelry and makeup.

Amish men cover their heads with broad-rimmed hats when they go outdoors. Hats are of black felt material in cold weather and straw in warmer weather. When dressed for church or formal occasions, men wear "plain suits." These suits do not have lapels and close with hooks and eyes rather than buttons. Suspenders are worn instead of belts. Men don white shirts for dress-up occasions and solid-colored shirts for work or casual wear. Shirts may have snap or button closures. After marriage, an Amish man grows an untrimmed beard but does not wear a mustache. Hair is parted in the middle and cropped in a bowl cut with bangs.

Language

Language reinforces group identity. "Pennsylvania Dutch," a German dialect, is used conversationally and is the first language for children. School, conducted in English, is a primary source for learning English. German is taught in school, but not used conversationally. Hymnbooks and Bibles are written in German. Church sermons are preached using a mixture of German and Pennsylvania Dutch, depending on the speaker. Amish people are familiar with using any of three languages - Pennsylvania Dutch, English, and German.

Church

Church services are held in the homes of members. A congregation typically comprises approximately thirty families living in close proximity. Leadership is shared between a bishop, a minister, and a deacon. These men, chosen from within the congregation, serve without formal training or salary. Services are held every other Sunday moving from home to home. Members of the congregation eat together following the morning preaching service.

Family Systems

Amish church and family systems are strongly patriarchal with men assuming leadership in most spheres. There is, however, a deep respect for women and the part they play in family life. Though roles are clearly defined, Amish society maintains a pattern of mutuality. Men shoulder most of the responsibilities associated with farming and fieldwork. Women oversee housework and gardening. Even with clearly defined duties, there is an understanding of companionship in the workload surrounding the home and farmstead. Women sometimes help in the barn and fields. It is equally likely that men participate in garden work. Many men work at home and are involved with childcare. Little girls and boys work side by side with parents and grandparents. Children soon learn the value and reward of hard work and a job well done.

Farms follow a daily rhythm that flows into weeks, months and years. Sunrise and sunset are the indicators for work and rest. Soil that is tilled and planted yields a harvest of food for both family and livestock. Respect for life and the cycle of the seasons is a natural outcome of working with the land. The Amish thank God for the abundance of the earth.

In a strongly patriarchal system, there is always the possibility of abuse. The Amish are not exempt. But generally, there is partnership rather than control and respect takes precedence over exploitation.

Technology

Amish do not avoid the advantages and rewards of modern technology. Rather, they make conscious choices to manage technology so that it does not infringe on the more highly prized values of family and community.

Amish have chosen to literally separate themselves from the world by avoiding connections to power lines. Amish homes operate efficiently and comfortably without tying into a public utility's electricity lines. Alternative energy sources — gas, diesel, battery, wind, hydraulic and pneumatic power — run farm equipment, kitchen appliances, washing machines and sewing machines.

The use of computers has been a troublesome issue for the Amish community. Though there are obvious advantages, many congregations have concluded that the potential distractions and temptations presented by computers and the Internet tip the scales in favor of avoiding their ownership. Television sets and radios are also taboo in Amish homes. Amish families stay up to date with news and current events by reading newspapers. Local libraries are frequented by Amish clientele. Reading materials in homes are selected to support the values and beliefs held by the church and family.

It is not unusual for Amish families to have a telephone. However, it is placed in a barn, garage, or phone booth some distance from the house, where it will not intrude on family time. With this arrangement, the family controls the phone rather than the phone controlling the family. The increase of cottage industries has made telephones important for conducting business. Many of these home enterprises deal with the issue through use of an answering machine that will take calls and allow response at the convenience of the receiver.

Horse-drawn carriages are the primary mode of transportation. It is a choice for a different pace of living. Individuals and groups will hire a vehicle and driver if necessary for trips to the doctor, to town, or for extended travel. Mostly, the horse and carriage limit the sphere of travel and dictate less frivolous "running around."

Education

Formal education takes place in Amish-owned one-room schools, where the basics of reading, writing, and arithmetic are emphasized. Curiosity is invited and encouraged. The purpose of education is to make one a practical member of the Amish community. Students attend school through Grade Eight, after which organized education is discontinued. Life skills go on being acquired in the routines of daily living. The ability to think critically and articulate exactly what one is thinking is not of high value in Amish culture. Learning to get along with one's family and neighbors is a more prized virtue.

Beauty and Function

It may seem ironic that stunningly bold quilts come from a group whose primary interests are simplicity and conformity. But the Amish have great appreciation for beauty. Lawns and gardens are carefully manicured and filled with an abundance of flowers. The beauty of sunrises and sunsets is not lost on a people whose daily rhythms follow the path of the sun. There is joy in the sprouting of a tender shoot of corn through the dark springtime soil and in the last fire-red leaf falling from a tree in autumn. Brilliant winter crystals and soft summer raindrops bring precious moisture to the earth. All this is watched and cherished as part of the beauty of God's created order.

Amish homes combine "plain" with "fancy." Corner cupboards are brimming with fancy dishes. Furniture may be decorated with lovely hand-painted accents. Family records ornamented with flowers and scenic landscapes list names and birth dates of children. The redeeming quality in these fancy objects is that they marry beauty and function. Beauty without function is of little worth. Function with beauty is enjoyed and celebrated.

Amish quilts fit this formula. They are works of love and function, blessed with beauty.

Amish girl tends the kitchen garden. Although men do the bulk of the field work, Amish women are responsible for the vegetables and fruits grown for use in the home. Their kitchen garden is also liberally planted with lovely flowers that bloom all summer long. *Image courtesy of PA Dutch Convention & Visitors Bureau.*

Opposite page: Amish children draw water for garden needs. Water pressure is maintained by the use of windmills and elevated storage tanks. *Image courtesy of PA Dutch Convention & Visitors Bureau.*

Amish children play on a farm wagon. *Photograph by Bruce Waters.*

Monday morning wash line on a Lancaster County, Pennsylvania, Amish farm. The towels and men's shirts show a variety of the colors acceptable within this Amish community. As indicated by the children's clothing, a large active family lives here. *Photograph by Bruce Waters.*

Amish women gather at a Saturday country auction in Lancaster County. *Photograph by Bruce Waters.*

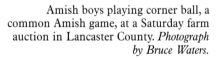

Amish boys playing corner ball, a common Amish game, at a Saturday farm auction in Lancaster County. *Photograph by Bruce Waters.*

Amish farmer and his mule team harvest corn. *Photograph by Bruce Waters.*

An Amish family out on a Lancaster County road in their horse-drawn carriage. This is their version of the family car. *Photograph by Bruce Waters.*

Amish men prepare produce for a Saturday country auction in Lancaster County. *Photograph by Bruce Waters.*

A one-room Amish schoolhouse in Lancaster County. It is complete with a fenced-in yard, outhouse, and a bell atop the building to signal school hours. *Photograph by Bruce Waters.*

An Amish boy inside a typical one-room Amish schoolhouse. *Image courtesy of Ron Bowman/ PA Dutch Convention & Visitors Bureau.*

An Amish family brings a portion of the tobacco harvest into the tobacco shed. Leaf tobacco is a labor-intensive but important cash crop for the Amish of Lancaster County. The cut tobacco seen here must be hung in a special type of barn to dry, then the leaf must be stripped from the stalk before it is baled and sold to tobacco buyers later in the winter. *Image courtesy of Ron Bowman/PA Dutch Convention & Visitors Bureau.*

A young Amish man drives his "courting buggy" on a busy Lancaster County, Pennsylvania highway. An unmarried man will use an open carriage, as seen here, but upon marriage will use an enclosed one. *Image courtesy of Ron Bowman/PA Dutch Convention & Visitors Bureau.*

Chapter 3

Understanding the Lancaster County Amish Quilt

History of the Pennsylvania German Bed

A brief history of the development of the quilt form within the Lancaster Amish community seems appropriate. Knowledge of the specific characteristics of the quilts of this particular settlement may be helpful as the reader looks closely at each example.

As you go through this process, be on guard! The same fervor and enthusiasm that led Doug Tompkins to amass these incredible textiles may compel you to collect or create similar pieces.

Like other members of the Pennsylvania German population who settled in southeastern Pennsylvania in the late 1600s and early 1700s, the Amish brought with them the traditions of their homeland. The typical Swiss bedcovering of that period would have been a woven spread, not a quilt.

Although nothing of this early period seems to have survived, there are examples of woven Amish bed coverings dating from the early 1800s. Seen in the first example is a hand woven coverlet made for Anna Kurtz (1820-99) by a professional Pennsylvania German weaver. Often referred to as a Star and Diamond pattern, it was woven on a typical multiple-shaft Pennsylvania German loom that produced cloth about 36 to 40 inches wide. The two pieces were sewn together to create a full bed width. Marked "A+K 1836," it was likely part of Anna Kurz's dowry before her marriage to Amish minister Jacob Stoltzfus.[1]

Anna, who was the third wife of Jacob, probably marked the coverlet herself with this red wool cross-stitching. Their bed and bedstead would have been similar to those in use in other Amish and non-Amish Pennsylvania German households of the period. A recreation of such a bed and bedstead is shown. A roped wooden bedstead supported a heaping pile of textiles, often referred to as the bed. On the bottom was a covered chaff bag filled with straw on which the sleepers lay. Over this might be only one handspun linen sheet. On top of this lay a feather tick enveloped in a decorative plaid linen cover on which rested the coverlet. Under the sleepers' heads were piled a long feather bolster with a case made of plaid linen, and on top of that two feather pillows and their covers. One can imagine that the sleepers were almost in a sitting position as they rested between the chaff bag and sheet.[2] It is not surprising that in many Pennsylvania estate inventories "the bed," or bedding textiles, constituted one of the most important and costly parts of the household.

Bed and bedding as it might have been seen in a Pennsylvania German home c. 1845. *Image courtesy of the Heritage Center of Lancaster County, Inc.*

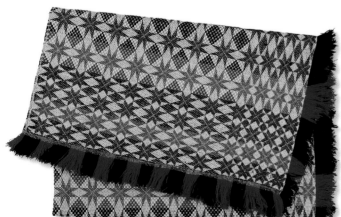

Star and Diamond pattern handwoven coverlet, initialed and dated "A x K 1836," for Lancaster County Amish owner Anna Kurtz, maker unknown. Twelve-shaft weave with center seam, cotton warp, wool and cotton weft, rolled top hem, self-fringed side edges, sewn-on wool and cotton bottom fringe, 78" x 97". *Private collection.*

The textiles making up the bed were consistently included in the traditional Pennsylvania German *Aussteier* or dowry.[3] Both women and men traditionally brought household objects to the marriage. Although in the Amish household the man's dowry was more likely to include a team of horses or other farm animals, it frequently contained furniture and quilts or spreads. Quilts in this case usually referred to the wool pieced bedcoverings that could not be washed. Spreads, on the other hand, were made of washable materials.[4] Although this tradition is a thing of the past in many Pennsylvania German households, the *Aussteier* tradition is still commonly practiced in Lancaster Amish families.

A later example of a woven blanket, possibly used for a less important bed in an Amish household, is pictured. Woven in the late 1800s, it also was done on a narrow loom and has a center seam similar to Anna Kurtz's coverlet. This piece of a simpler twill weave was worked on a multicolored cotton warp similar to that used for strip carpeting so commonly seen in Amish homes. As coverlets and handwoven linens went out of favor in Amish homes, local weavers might have made an occasional blanket but spent most of their time manufacturing carpet in order to make a living. Such carpet is still being made and used in Amish homes in the twenty-first century.

Handwoven blanket, Lancaster County, Pennsylvania Amish, maker unknown, c. 1880. Twill weave with center seam, cotton warp, wool weft, twill tape top binding, self-fringed bottom edge, 72" x 74". *Private collection.*

Also found in old Amish estate sales and homes are Jacquard-patterned coverlets woven by professional weavers in the community. These were usually made in a factory-like setting, and they were inexpensive enough to replace the individually produced bed coverings. The child's coverlet shown here, produced in the late 1800s, was found in a Lancaster County Amish home.

Amish child's coverlet, Lancaster County, maker unknown, c. 1880. Wool and cotton Jacquard-patterned weave, 41" square. *Gift of George Lyster in memory of Kimberly Ann Bupp to the Heritage Center of Lancaster County, Inc.*

By this time in the 1870s, weavers were not able to compete with manufactured bedding and inexpensive fabrics available for clothing and piecing into quilts. It appears that Amish women were adapting to the quilt-making ways of their "English"[5] neighbors. By the mid 1880s Amish women's diaries recorded many hours spent in quilting.[6]

Although a great deal of hand sewing was being done, the sewing machine was quickly adopted by women in the Amish community as a welcome laborsaving device. In 1886 Rebecca Lapp, a thirteen-year-old Amish girl, recorded in her diary, "Cloudy all day we sewed morning Lizzie and Mother went to Vogansville to Daniel Weaver for a sewing machine."[7] This of course would have been a treadle machine, a type still being used in the non-electrified homes of the Amish. The majority of quilts we associate with the Lancaster Amish, and those in this collection, are machine pieced.

Lancaster County Amish Quilt Patterns

There are only a limited number of traditional patterns associated with Lancaster Amish quiltmaking. The major ones are Center Square, Diamond in the Square, Sunshine and Shadow, Bars, and a small variety of Block pattern quilts. But there are many interesting variations used within these patterns that are well illustrated by examples in the collection. The introductory section the Pellmans have written in this book provide insight into the importance of conformity within the Lancaster Amish community and its families. Being aware of the value systems within which Amish quilters work will help the reader understand why there were relatively limited patterns produced.

A few generalizations about measurements and proportions will help separate Lancaster Amish quilts from those made by their "English" neighbors and by Amish in other communities. The majority of the early patterns are square or nearly so. However, the 1875 Amish Center Square is an exception, as it is longer than it is wide. Some of the Bars pattern quilts are not square, particularly the more idiosyncratic and the later examples. More recent pieced-block patterns, reflecting the influence of non-Amish quilting traditions, are often rectangular. But in looking at these patterns in the collection (Nine Patch, Irish Chain, Baskets, and Crazy quilts) one notices that this too is not a hard-and-fast rule.

Center Square quilt, eastern Lancaster County, Amish, initialed and dated in the quilting "GD/1875," maker unknown. Top: plain-weave wool; back: brown plain-weave cotton, 82" x 85". *Private collection.*

The outer borders of the Lancaster quilts are proportionally wider than quilts from other Amish communities. When they have corner blocks, those, by necessity of design, are larger and often have bold contrasting colors. The quilts themselves are of relatively modest proportions. The average dimensions range from about 70 inches to 85 inches, most within a narrower range. Few crib- or child-size quilts have survived in the Lancaster Amish community, although they are more common in the Midwest settlements. All of the quilts, with a few exceptions (illustrated by Plates 18 and 78) are finished off with a wide (1 to 1.5- inch) binding, discussed in more detail later.

Early Amish Quilts and Possible Origins

The Amish Center Square quilt is initialed and dated "GD/1875." This is one of the few dated examples of a Lancaster Amish quilt of this period. One must assume that these few pieced-wool quilts, based on a Center Medallion design, are representative of a type first being made by Amish women in Lancaster County. In most cases, the earlier Lancaster Amish quilts (those made before 1920) are central framed motifs using large pieces of material. Thus we identify such commonly known early patterns as Center Square, Rectangle, Diamond, and Bars. All of these patterns are well represented in the collection.

Although similar plain quilts having a Center Medallion design were not common in other Pennsylvania German households of the time, the general pattern does relate to a few known Quaker quilts of an earlier period. The quilt shown next is a Center Square variation signed and dated "Rachel/Taylor/1811." Rachel was a Quaker woman living in a rural area of Bradford Township, central Chester County. Note that Chester County shares a common border with the southeastern portion of Lancaster County where significant numbers of Amish had settled by this time. The Quaker quilt is also pieced from wools, but they are of a coarser glazed fabric typical of manufacture at this earlier date. The resemblance of the general quilt format and quilting patterns of Lancaster County Amish quilts to some nineteenth century Welsh quilts has also been suggested.[8] There were Welsh settlers in the eastern end of Lancaster County, known as the Welsh Mountains.

Center Square variation, Quaker quilt, Chester County, Pennsylvania, signed with orange wool chain-stitch by the maker "Rachel/Taylor/ 1811." Top: plain-weave glazed wool; filling: unspun and undyed wool; back: wool and cotton, 97" x 103". *Collection of Warren and Christine Reynolds, photograph by brt Photographic Illustrations.*

Pattern Development

Every effort to neatly categorize groups brings up some exceptions. The Log Cabin quilt is just such an exception. Although not dated, its fabrics suggest it was made in the late nineteenth century. The wools, batting, and cotton backing are similar to those in the dated 1875 Center Square. The Log Cabin pattern is rarely found in fine-quality Amish bed quilts. (There are none in the Esprit collection.) It was occasionally used later in the 1900s by Amish women to make comforters. This pattern, on the other hand, was widely used by other Pennsylvania German women and American women from many other backgrounds and locations.

Log Cabin quilt, eastern Lancaster County, Amish, maker unknown, c. 1900. Top: plain-weave, twill-weave, patterned-weave, and printed wool; back: plain-weave brown-and-white printed cotton, 85" square. *Private collection.*

An interesting aspect of the quilt is the insertion of two "logs" of printed fabric. Printed fabric is seldom used on the top surface of a Lancaster Amish quilt.[9] Looking closely at the quilt, one notes that the wide border surrounding the central pieced area is filled with the typical feather quilting pattern seen in most Lancaster County Amish quilts of this early period. But as a finishing touch an unusually narrow contrasting binding was applied, outlining nontraditional rounded corners. One wonders what the maker of this unusual quilt was thinking as she created such a bold masterpiece.

This unusual display of individuality is not the norm in the tradition-bound Amish society of Lancaster County. A high rating is placed on community values, and the individual's personal feelings are subordinate to the good of the general community. As a result, there appears outwardly less obvious expression of individuality. This is reflected in the general homogeneity of clothing, decorative effects, and household goods within the Amish home.[10]

In the late 1920s and into the 1930s, a few other less common Lancaster County Amish patterns occur that seem to break with the Medallion style. They also appear to have been borrowed from "English" neighbors. Examples can be noted in the block-design patterns known as Fans, Baskets, Nine Patch, and Double Nine Patch and their variations. A number of examples found their way into the collection. But the origins of the basic Center Square and large Medallion designs found so commonly within the Lancaster County Amish community have yet to be fully explored.

Also in the 1920s the use of smaller blocks within the large Medallion format became popular with Lancaster Amish quilters. The resulting pattern, seen in Plates 29-37, is now called Sunshine and Shadow with its many variations. These too are well represented in the collection. The same pattern was commonly used by Lancaster Mennonite women starting in the late 1800s. Although the pattern was the same, the Mennonites usually executed it in cottons instead of wools, using small-design printed fabrics. Their name for a variation of this pattern is Trip Around the World. Compare this with the Amish quilt illustrated in Plate 28, here classified as a Diamond in the Square—Sunshine and Shadow variation.

Center Diamond—Trip Around the World variation, made for Dorothy Ann Groff by her Lancaster County, Mennonite grandmother, Frances Keen (Mrs. Zephaniah) Binkley, 1928. Top: Plain-weave printed cotton; back: plain-weave printed cotton strips, 80" square. *Gift of Dorothy A. Groff in memory of Frances Keen Binkley to the Heritage Center of Lancaster County, Inc.*

One might ask why Lancaster Amish women did not create appliquéd quilts. Again, the strong communal influence over individual tastes and expression comes into play. With that said, the exceptional Four Block Tulip appliquéd quilt needs to be considered. To the author's knowledge this is one of only a few fully developed appliquéd Lancaster Amish quilts made before 1940 for use within the community. It is likely that some Amish women were appliquéing with or for their English neighbors. This unusual example was purchased from an Amish home by a local Lancaster quilt dealer who was told it had been made by Katie Zook, who lived in Leola, Lancaster County, for use by her family.[11] A similar quilt, with slightly different color distribution, has also been attributed to Katie.[12]

Four-Block Tulip appliquéd quilt, made by Katie Zook, an Amish woman living in Leola, Lancaster County, c. 1935. Top: plain-weave, twill-weave, and crepe wool; back: black-and-white checked and plaid plain-weave cotton, 84" square. *Private collection.*

The feather quilting pattern in the outer blue border is exactly what one would expect to see on a Lancaster County Amish quilt. The quilting within the sashing is similar to later 1930s or 1940s patterns found in the inner borders of more traditional patterns. The use of a waffle pattern over each tulip block, with no regard to the outline of the appliqué, appears stiff and, although well-executed, rather clumsy. This suggests that Katie was unfamiliar with her approach. Although it is technically well-constructed, the pattern lacks the flowing creative form and deft execution of a fine appliqué quilt.

The quilt shows little evidence of use. That is common with many of the finest Amish bedcoverings. Often they were saved for special events and taken from the blanket chest only to show to visiting friends and relatives. One might think that this piece was so out of the ordinary that it might not have been displayed because it would have drawn too much attention to the maker. What, one wonders, was going through this woman's mind as she planned and made this odd bedcovering?

Fabrics

Much has been written about the fabrics used in Lancaster County Amish quilts.[13] A great many misconceptions have found their way into the body of work written on the subject. In most cases the fabrics for the fine quilts made by Lancaster Amish women were not remnants from scrap bags, recycled clothing, or leftovers from other sewing projects. The fine dark wool fabrics seen in the early Lancaster quilt tops were made from yard goods purchased by the wife and mother when she was determining what materials were needed to make everyday and Sunday clothing and other household projects. At that time she made a conscious decision to purchase fabrics for use in quilts as well as her other household needs. Sources for fabrics were varied, depending on access, cost, and the time frame in which the sewing needed to be done. Mail order catalogs, department stores in the City of Lancaster and other local towns, and traveling peddlers—who purchased end lots from Philadelphia and New York—were all sources of quilting and clothing materials.[14]

Until the 1940s the tops made were almost exclusively of wool. As wools became more difficult to find, substitution of cottons and synthetic, or synthetic mixes, became popular. This is particularly evident in the Sunshine and Shadow pattern variations, as they are made up of so many different selections of fabric and they seemed to become among the most popular patterns from the 1940s on.

The wool fabrics used in the earliest quilts were twill- and plain-weave textiles. Wool crepes appear in the later 1930s quilts. Crepe fabrics, whether they were made of wool or rayon (both common Amish quilt fabrics), were produced using a tightly twisted fiber. The resulting surface of the woven cloth took on a crinkled look. Many descriptions of Amish quilts use the word "crepe" synonymously with rayon. This is not correct. Crepe can be of either content. Along with the crepe wools, a variety of rayon crepes and cotton fabrics were introduced. By the 1940s all of these fabrics were in common use, replacing the older wool materials.

The colors of these top fabrics also changed with time. Early quilts tended to have less color variety. The Center Square, shown earlier, only two colors. Brown and darker shades of blues are greens were predominant in pre-1900 examples. Contrary to what has been published in the literature, few if any of these early Lancaster quilts were homespun or home-dyed. By the 1870s commercially manufactured fabrics were available and affordable to the Amish residents of Lancaster County.

Later in the 1930s hot pinks and bright lavenders appeared, along with other lighter colors. Although uncommon, black was occasionally used in Lancaster quilts. Bold and vivid red, blue, turquoise, green, and purple were expertly combined by Amish women from the 1920s on. Occasionally in later 1930s and 1940s quilts, one sees small blocks of pale yellow and white, but not in overwhelming quantity. By mid-century colors and patterns were changing so radically that the traditional Lancaster Amish quilt, as we know it, was less frequently produced by Amish quilters even for their own use. The Ribbon quilt pictured next was probably made between 1940 and 1960. One can see the underlying influence of the Medallion format, but innovations such as decorative needlework and appliqué have been introduced, and the deep saturated colors have been abandoned.

Ribbon quilt, maker unknown, Amish, Lancaster Co., c. 1950. Top: paint, cotton embroidery floss, plain-weave cotton; back: white plain-weave cotton; fringe: commercially woven synthetic fiber, 79.5" x 84". *Gift of George Lyster in memory of Kimberly Ann Bupp to the Heritage Center of Lancaster County, Inc.*

Filling

Thin cotton batting as the filling, or intermediary layer, in these best quilts appears to have been continually used from the earliest period well into the 1940s. Rarely is wool batting found in a Lancaster County, Pa. Amish quilt. The emphasis on small, evenly and closely placed quilting stitches has always been strong among Lancaster County Amish quilters. The thin batting made this possible. With the introduction of polyester filling material, even the best quilters could not mimic the earlier quilting style.

Quilting Patterns

Quilting patterns also changed over the years. Examining the outside borders in quilts within the collection points out certain gradual changes. The classic and early feather pattern persisted throughout the period these quilts were being made. Earlier examples appear more densely quilted, containing bolder curving lines and extra fill in quilted areas. A pattern resembling fern fronds is also seen on early examples. Motifs such as baskets of fruit and flowers were introduced; and later, grape and rose vines, less tightly quilted, filled these border areas.

Binding

Edge treatment throughout the production of these quilts remained the same. As examples in the collection are analyzed, it becomes evident that binding widths consistently measure between 1 and 1.5 inches and that they extend beyond the body of the quilt. The binding was usually applied by machine on the face of the quilt and then either machine or hand finished on the back. Examples of typical bindings are shown next. Two notable exceptions are pictured in Plates 18 and 78. The usual corners are square, but again Plate 18 is an exception.

Detail of corner edges showing top and back surfaces of two Lancaster County Amish quilts. Bottom quilt was applied by machine on the front surface, then turned and finished by hand on the back. The top quilt also was applied by machine on the front surface, then finished by machine on the back.

Backing

And now for the last, least discussed, and almost never photographed aspect of Lancaster Amish quilts. What about the quilt back? Throughout the book, as we investigate each piece, there has been an attempt to show details of a number of backing materials: the plain, the bold, the figured, and the unexpected. Amish women chose a wide variety of fabrics. Almost all were cottons, and seldom was a large-scale print used. The reasons for choice were of course acceptance within community standards and, probably most pressing, the cost, availability, and suitability of the fabric itself. It will become apparent to the reader that there was indeed some consistency even in this unseen choice. The next picture illustrates examples of plain and figured backing materials.

As the quilts are described in the captions accompanying the Plates, two aspects have been almost completely ignored because they are so consistent. The color of the quilting thread is usually black; and the middle layer, or filling, is usually a thin layer of cotton batting. When there is a variation it is noted.

Some general comments might be kept in mind while viewing the quilts pictured in this book. Occasional discrepencies in color found in multiple images of a single quilt are due to the photographs being taken at different times under varying light conditions. Quilt measurements have been taken as accurately as possible, but the properties of cloth and the process of creating quilts defies total mathematical perfection. We hope that the dimensions given will give the reader a better understanding of the pictures as real objects and will be helpful for those wishing to create pieces of their own. In exploring and analyzing the individual quilts, we in no way are judging the work of the talented women who created them.

With these brief guidelines in mind, it is time to go forth and enjoy these beautiful Lancaster Amish quilts!

[1] Gingerich, Hugh R., and Kreider, Rachel W., *Amish and Amish Mennonite Genealogies* (Gordonville, Pa.: Pequea Publishers, 1986), 229.
[2] See Alan Keyser, "Beds, Bedding, Bedsteads and Sleep," *Der Reggebogge (The Rainbow)*, quarterly of the Pennsylvania German Society 12:4 (1978), 1-28.
[3] An excellent book explaining this fascinating tradition has been written by Jeannette Lasansky: *A Good Start: the Aussteier or Dowry* (Lewisburg, Pa.: Oral Traditions Project, 1990).
[4] Lasansky, *A Good Start*, discusses several Lancaster Amish dowries in detail, 30-37.
[5] "English" is a general term that Amish people use to refer to any non-Amish person.
[6] See Kraybill, Herr, and Holstein, *A Quiet Spirit: Amish Quilts from the Collection of Cindy Tietze & Stuart Hodosh* (Los Angeles: UCLA Fowler Museum of Cultural History, 1996), 52-53, as one example charting the textile production of Susan S. Lapp as reflected in her 1886 diary.
[7] Rebecca Lapp diary, November 11, 1886. Private collection.
[8] Jonathan Holstein in his essay section of Kraybill, Herr, and Holstein, *A Quiet Spirit*, 82-83, makes this suggestion.
[9] One other similar Log Cabin pattern Lancaster County Amish quilt with the same discrepancy is known to the author. Very likely it is the work of the same woman or a family member. This quilt is in a private collection.
[10] This concept is discussed in depth in the works of two noted Amish scholars and authors, John A. Hostetler and Donald B. Kraybill, cited in the bibliography included in this book.
[11] From personal communication with Frances Woods, the dealer who originally purchased the quilt from a Lancaster Amish family.
[12] A description of the quilt is contained in a letter written to Esprit curator Julie Silber by collector and author Daniel J. McCauley dated "13 April 89." The location of the quilt is unknown.
[13] For an excellent discussion of the fabric used in Lancaster Amish quilts, see Eve Wheatcroft Granick, *The Amish Quilt* (Intercourse, Pa.: Good Books, 1989), 41-57.
[14] Granick in *The Amish Quilt* 57-72, gives a detailed listing, complete with period advertisements, of the options Lancaster Amish women had in purchasing these materials.

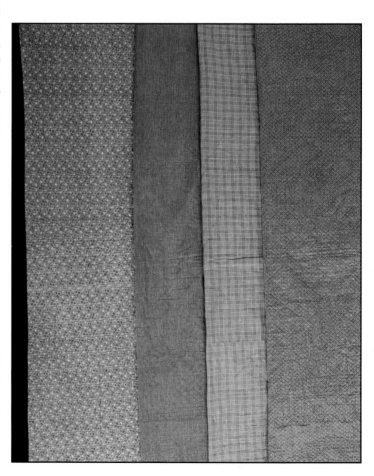

Detail of the backs of four Lancaster County Amish quilts. From left to right the cotton fabrics are a multicolor floral printed material, a plain-weave blue-and-white chambray, a plain-weave lavender-and-white woven plaid, and a black-and-white pattern-woven material.

Chapter 4
The Quilt Collection

Center Square

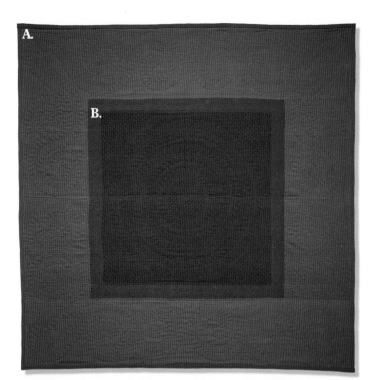

Overall dimensions: 78" square
Binding: 1"
Outer border: 15.5
Inner border: 3"
Center square: 39"

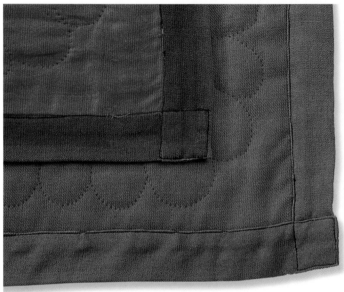

A. Detail of corner binding and back: The bindings of the majority of the Amish quilts in this collection were attached by machine but turned and finished by hand. Some, like this example, were all machine-sewn. The choice of technique does not seem to correlate with the age of the quilt. Most surviving Amish quilts were made after the invention and wide distribution of the sewing machine. It is not surprising that Amish needleworkers were quick to adopt the new treadle machine as a valuable labor-saving device. Theirs was a culture that encouraged the home manufacture of most clothing and bedding, and this was time-consuming even after the introduction of the sewing machine.

B. Detail of three top wool materials: Pictured here are the three fine twill-weave wool fabrics used in the top of this early quilt. The quilt maker would have used similar fabrics for family clothing manufacture. The seams are joined with machine stitching but quilted by hand with fine, regular, dark-colored quilting stitches typical of Lancaster County Amish quilts. The added scalloping on both sides of the inner border further adorns the surface of this admirably quilted example.

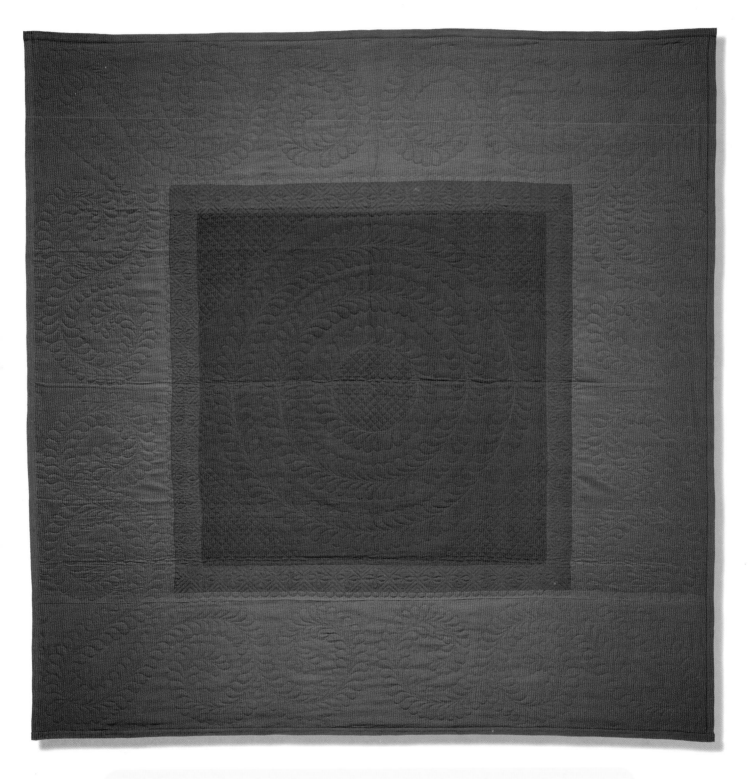

Plate 1
Center Square. Top: twill-weave wool; back: soft red twill-weave cotton; c. 1895. The Center Square is perhaps the simplest and most elegant pattern made by Lancaster County Amish women. Quilts of this form are among the earliest found in the Lancaster community.

Center Square

Overall dimensions: 77" square
Binding: 1.5"
Outer border: 14"
Inner border: 4"
Center square: 38"

A. Detail of inner border: The four-petal flower surrounded by geometric diamond quilting is a pattern frequently used for inner borders in Lancaster County Amish quilts. This pattern has often been referred to as "pumpkin seed" quilting. Compared to the more static example in Plate 1, the petals in this quilt have an asymmetry suggesting the blades of a windmill.

B. Detail of back: Some Lancaster County Amish quilts are pieced from more than one fabric. This backing is interesting because the large central portion is made from a tan twill-weave wool, and the two narrower outer edges are a lighter shade of cotton sateen. Note that the binding has been applied with machine stitching.

Plate 2
Center Square. Top: twill-weave wool; back: brown twill-weave wool and sateen cotton; c. 1895. The bold red wool Center Square would suggest that this quilt was made slightly later than the quilt in Plate 1.

Center Square

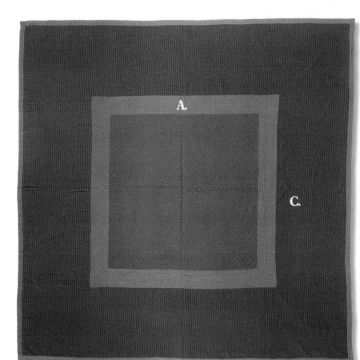

Overall dimensions: 77.5" square
Binding: 1.25
Outer border: 16
Inner border: 4.25
Center square: 34

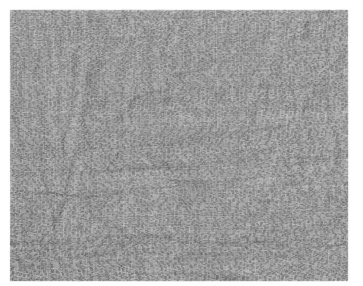

B. Detail of back: The brown-and-white woven-pattern cotton back is a type of material frequently used for backing Lancaster County Amish quilts. This would not have been a fabric used in family clothing.

A. Detail of inner border at top center: The appearance of straight-feather quilting is a departure from the more commonly seen floral and diamond pattern used in the previous examples. Notice the small dot quilted into the open space between the feather ends. The added scalloped quilting on each side is similar to that seen in Plate 1.

C. The curves in the outer feather border are elongated and squeezed until almost touching to create oval shapes instead of the more common round feather swirls.

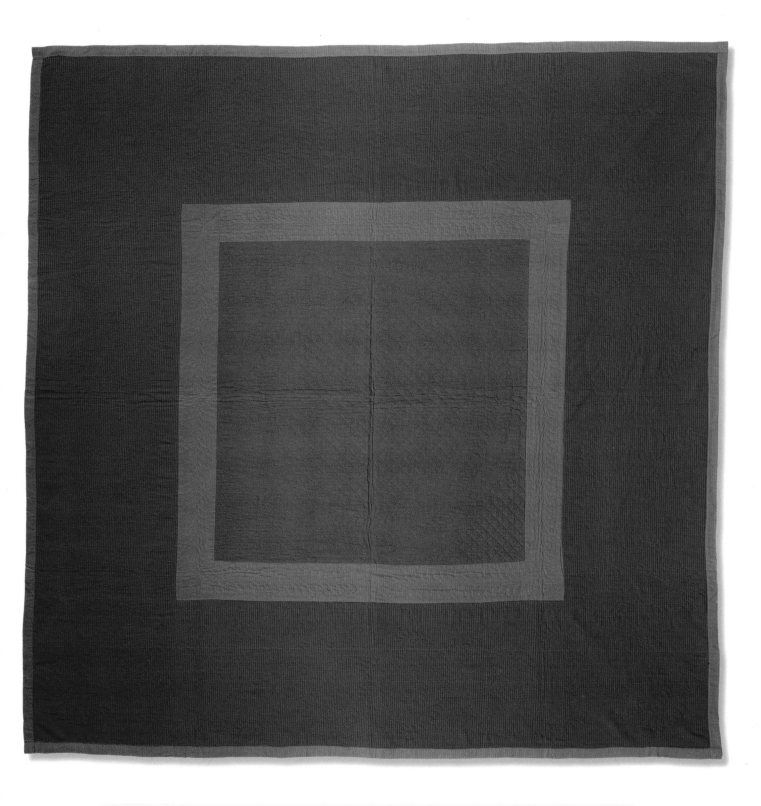

Plate 3

Center Square. Top: twill- and plain-weave wool; back: brown-and-white woven-plaid, plain-weave cotton; c. 1895. Seeing three similar examples of the simple Center Square pattern suggests that it was a common Lancaster County Amish quilt. They are quite rare and are considered by some collectors to be among the earliest and most desirable quilt form. Although these first three quilts appear to be similar, this example differs significantly in some of its quilting patterns. Note that the Center Square uses the same quilting patterns as the previous examples but in a slightly different arrangement. *Gift of Irene N. Walsh.*

Center Square

Overall dimensions: 74" square
Binding: 1.25"
Outer border: 12.75"
Inner border: 4"
Center square: 38"

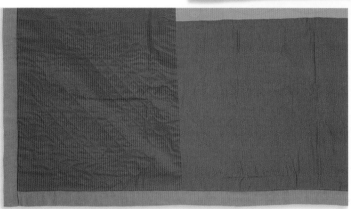

A. Detail of outer border at corner: Basket quilting in the outer borders is usually associated with quilts made in the 1920s and 1930s. Some examples, like these along the green border, appear to be fruit-filled and have coiled handles, making them more interesting than a simple basket outline would be. The red corner blocks are filled with fine wreath quilting.

B. Detail of inner border at corner: The selection of turquoise for use as an inner border brightens this quilt considerably and sets it apart from the previous examples, whose tonal range is not nearly so striking. The cable quilting with corner flowers is a later and less common inner-border quilting pattern.

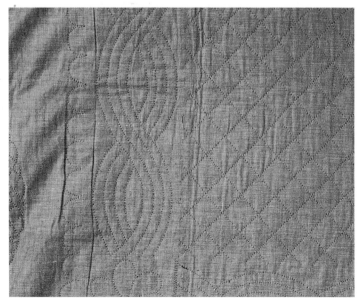

C. Detail of back: Chambray is defined as a plain-weave cotton material in which the warp and weft threads are of different colors. In this case they are black-and-white. Chambray is frequently used as backing in Lancaster County Amish quilts.

Plate 4

Center Square. Top: plain- and twill-weave wool; back: black-and-white plain-weave cotton chambray; c. 1920. This quilt is notable because of the added corner blocks. Although Center Square is considered to be an early pattern, the addition of corner blocks, the color of turquoise, and the simpler and less fluid quilting patterns suggest a later date for this quilt. The quilt was purchased from a farm near Peach Bottom in southern Lancaster County, an area still heavily populated with Amish farmers and their families.[1]

Diamond in the Square

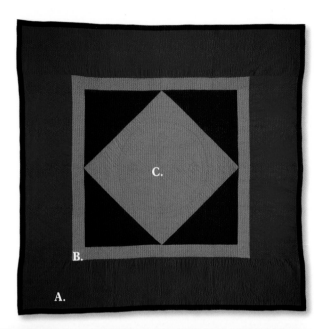

Overall dimensions: 81" square
Binding: 1.5"
Outer border: 13.5"
Inner border: 3.5"
Center square: 44"
Center diamond: 31"

A. Detail of outer border: The addition of a tulip at the end of each feather frond adds to the complexity of the quilting pattern and insures there is little open space within the outer border.

B. Detail of the pieced corner star: Three of the small corner stars are double-line quilted. This one is quilted with only a single line. Notice how a small portion on one side of the corner block is pieced, perhaps due to a minor measuring miscalculation rather than a shortage of fabric.

C. Although none of the previous quilts featured central star quilting, it is commonly seen in the center of the Diamond in the Square pattern.

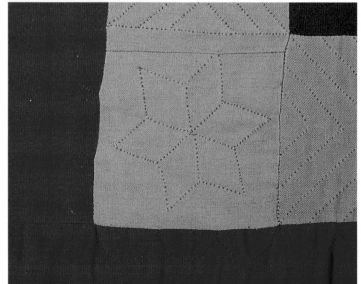

Plate 5

Diamond in the Square. Top: plain- and twill-weave wool; back: black-and-white plain-weave cotton chambray; c 1910. This pattern is considered by most collectors to be the classic Lancaster County Amish quilt design. Diamond in the Square, Bars, and Sunshine and Shadow quilts are considered the "big three" categories in this quilt genre. They are well represented in the group of 82 Esprit quilts but not found in overwhelming quantities as they would be in the general population of Lancaster County Amish quilts. The use of dark colors in similar tones would suggests that this quilt was made early in the twentieth century.

Diamond in the Square

Overall dimensions: 78" square
Binding: 1"
Outer border: 12"
Inner border: 4.5"
Center square: 43"
Center diamond: 31"

A. Detail of binding and back: This binding was initially applied to the body of the quilt with machine stitching, then was turned and hand-finished. The majority of the examples in this collection were done in the same manner. The choice of finishing process does not seem to relate to the age of the quilt. The back in this case is the commonly used plain-weave cotton chambray. In this case there are two tones of blue and a white fiber; when blended they provide the frosted appearance so popular in Amish quilts and clothing.

B. The quilting in this section is consistent with what was done in the rest of the quilt. No area escaped the quilter's needle. A single star has been placed in the open space between each point of the larger central star. Scalloping also fills the outer border of the blue block surrounding the central wreath.

Plate 6

Diamond in the Square. Top: plain- and twill-weave wool; back: blue-and-white plain-weave cotton chambray; c 1900. The quilting patterns in the outer and inner borders, corner triangles, and center block areas are classic and suggest that the quilt was made in the early 1900s. The relatively subdued colors in this piece also help date it to this period. The consistency of the elegant quilting is noteworthy. This is a hallmark of most Lancaster County Amish quilts. It was not uncommon for the woman who pieced the quilt to invite the most accomplished of her friends to take part in the quilting process.

Diamond in the Square

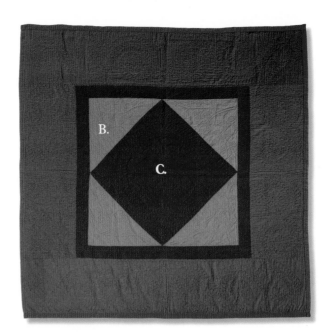

Overall dimensions: 75" square
Binding: 1.5"
Outer border: 13.75"
Inner border: 3.25"
Center square: 38"
Center diamond: 27"

A. Detail of the back: The printed cottons used for backing material simulate a twill-weave fabric. Two different fabrics, in one large and one small piece, have been joined to complete the back. This type of fabric was commonly used for backing material, but because of the pattern would not have been used by the Lancaster County Amish for clothing or quilt tops.

B. The rose and tulip branch quilting pattern seen in the turquoise triangles is consistent with a later period. Although the quilting is even and fine, it is slightly later than the traditional waffle pattern seen in the previous Diamond in the Square patterns.

C. The quilting is elegant and dense. Note the scalloping around the outer edge and the insertion of a bunch of grapes in each corner. The intricate quilting patterns add to the sculptural effect and impact of this example.

Plate 7
Diamond in the Square. Top: plain- and twill-weave wool; back: gray-and-white twill-print, plain-weave cotton; c. 1925. The use of turquoise wool in the center triangles suggests that this quilt was made in the 1920s or later. *Gift of Irene N. Walsh.*

Diamond in the Square

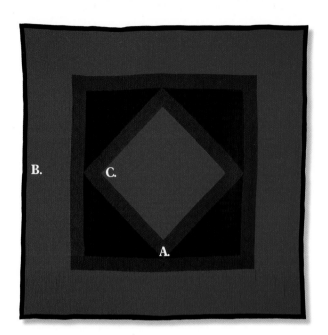

Overall dimensions: 78" square
Binding: 1.25"
Outer border: 12"
Both inner borders: 3.75"
Center square: 43.5"
Center diamond: 25"

A. Detail of inner square and diamond borders: A less common cable pattern has been used here in triple rows to fill and give dimension to the narrow purple strips. The corners are executed with a floral motif. The purple wool used here is woven from warp and weft threads of different colors, in this case purple and white. It is often referred to as henrietta cloth by the Amish.

B. So that few empty spaces would survive, the quilt maker added separate curved feather strips wherever there was room for them. With the same eye for adornment, she executed a scalloped pattern around the inner border edge adjoining the purple inner border.

C. Open areas were not to be tolerated by the expert quilter, and balanced double-stitched foliate devices fill in each red corner. These motifs are similar to the ones quilted into the corners of the center diamond of the quilt pictured in Plate 14.

Plate 8

Diamond in the Square. Top: twill-weave wool; back: black sateen-weave cotton; c. 1925. Another element of design, the second narrow inner border surrounding the diamond, has been added. Typically in this arrangement it is the same width as the narrow square inner border. The bold red center and outer border make this type of quilt most desirable to collectors of Lancaster County Amish quilts. *Gift of Irene N. Walsh.*

Diamond in the Square

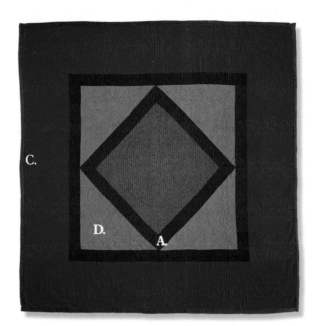

Overall dimensions: 76" square
Binding: 1.25"
Outer border: 12.5"
Both inner borders: 3.25"
Center square: 42"
Center diamond: 24"

A. Detail of narrow purple borders: The grapevine pattern used in both narrow purple inner borders is most commonly seen in quilts made in the later 1920s and 1930s.

B. Detail of the back: As noted before the small-motif printed cottons of just two colors were frequently used by Amish women as backing materials but not in their clothing or quilt tops.

C. Although the usual feather quilting in the outer red border is not as dense as found on some earlier quilts, the quilter has made an attempt to fill in open areas with a floral device.

D. The branching rose and tulip quilting pattern is also typical of the later 1920s and 1930s. In this case the quilter has taken the time to double-stitch the motif. Here on the lighter turquoise ground the finely quilted black thread is easily seen.

Plate 9
Diamond in the Square. Top: plain- and twill-weave wool; back: maroon-and-white printed plain-weave cotton; c 1925. This classic wool Diamond in the Square quilt is pieced from a pleasing selection of intense colors that might have been used earlier in the century, but the rose motif quilting in the turquoise field suggests a mid-1920s date or later.

Diamond in the Square

Overall dimensions: 84.5" square
Binding: 1.25"
Outer border: 13"
Both inner borders: 3.75"
Center square: 48.5"
Center diamond: 27.5"

A. Detail of inner border corner block and green triangular block: The choice of such a light color is unusual in Lancaster County Amish quilts and might suggest a later innovation. The quilting thread is consistently black with no effort to match the light color of the top fabric. The slightly later rose motif was quilted in the triangular area. It does not provide the dense sculptural effect of the fine earlier waffle quilting.

B. Detail of center from the back: The open floral quilting throughout the red center is also a departure from the more common and geometric star and wreath. This too suggests a quilt made in the later 1930s. The backing material is a simple plain-weave blue cotton.

Plate 10
Diamond in the Square. Top: plain- and crepe-weave wool; back: blue plain-weave cotton; c. 1935. The appearance of corner blocks within the narrow inner border adds some complexity to the pattern, but it is not as developed as the following quilts, which have large corner blocks in the wide outer border. This innovation suggests a slightly later development in the Diamond in the Square pattern, as does the larger size.

Diamond in the Square

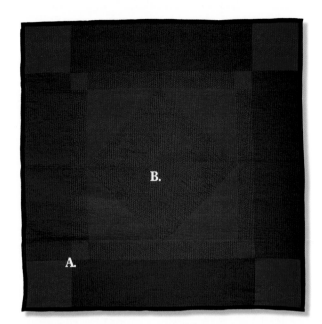

Overall dimensions: 76.5" square
Binding: 1.25"
Outer border: 12.5"
Inner border: 4.5"
Center square: 40"
Center diamond: 28.75"

A. Detail of outer and inner corner block: Although the area of the outer corner block is not densely quilted the well-executed compote of fruit is outstanding and unusual. The inner corner block contains a simple but effective flower motif that is cleverly constructed of four outward-facing tulips.

B. Detail of central area from the back: The well-designed and executed quilting motifs continue through the diamond in another variation of the star and wreath we have seen before in this pattern.

Plate 11
Diamond in the Square. Top: plain-weave wool; back: blue-and-white plain-weave cotton chambray; c. 1925. This quilt introduces the more complex arrangement that includes corner blocks in the wide outer border. The red color progression from large outer block to smaller red inner block, then connecting to the red field is a particularly effective design and one that makes this one of the outstanding examples of its genre. *Gift of Irene N. Walsh.*

Diamond in the Square

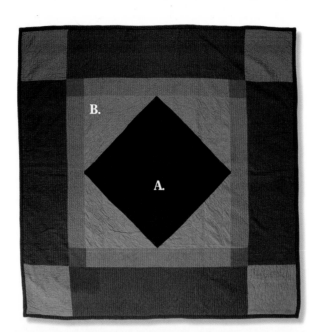

Overall dimensions: 74" square
Binding: 1.25"
Outer border: 12"
Inner border: 4.5"
Center square: 38.5"
Center diamond: 27.75"

A. Detail of center diamond from the back: In the dark center diamond area the quilting patterns are more easily seen from the back of the quilt. Flannel was frequently used by the Amish as a backing; it was a seemingly commonplace fabric to back such an elegant quilt. The printed pattern simulates a twill-weave fabric. This type of fabric was a popular choice among Amish women. The quilter has added an interesting double-stitched floral device to fill open areas in each corner of the central diamond.

B. The light background color of the area allows us to better see the quilting patterns. The quilter has chosen to place two stars on each side of the upper and lower points of the center square. Although a bit askew, they fill in the small bit of open space not occupied by the rose and tulip branch design.

Plate 12
Diamond in the Square. Top: plain- and twill-weave wool; back: green twill-weave cotton flannel; c. 1925. The more subtle shades of fabric chosen imbue this quilt with a calming peaceful effect. The fabric used in the dark center is a fine example of a wool henrietta cloth. The maker's daughter remembers this as "the dark blue from my mother's dress."[2]

Diamond in the Square

Overall dimensions: 79" square
Binding: 1.25"
Outer border: 11.25."
Inner border: 3.75"
Center square: 46.5"
Diamond border: 3.5"
Center Diamond: 26"

A. Detail of inner border: The rayon crepe has a much shinier hard surface typical of the early synthetic fabrics. The grapevine quilting pattern was used in both narrow blue borders.

B. The rather stiff open floral quilting patterns seen here are associated with later quilts. One sees more geometric densely quilted flowing patterns in earlier examples. The blue corner-block fabric is a woolen crepe, also suggesting a 1930s or 1940s quilt. Compare this with the shiny rayon crepe used in the narrow purple inner border.

Plate 13
Diamond in the Square. Top: plain-weave and crepe wool and rayon; back: green plain-weave cotton; c. 1940. Bright colors and the inclusion of rayon fabrics place this quilt's origin close to 1940, when rayon had become generally available.

Diamond in the Square

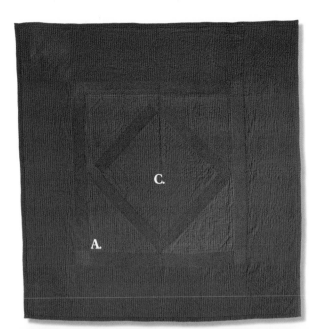

Overall dimensions: 78" square
Binding: 1.25"
Outer border: 13.75"
Inner border: 3.5"
Center square: 41"
Diamond border: 3.5"
Center diamond: 23"

A. Detail of triangle: For the triangular blocks the quilter chose an interesting combination of double quilted flower motifs flanking a fruit-filled basket. Fine and even quilting is consistent with the dating of this piece.

B. Detail of back: As in the quilt shown in Plate 12, flannel was chosen as a backing. The woven pattern, using a white thread as a regularly repeated warp thread, adds interest to the textile.

C. Another form of a bilaterally symmetrical foliate device was added to the points of the diamond to fill in unquilted space. These appear to be similar to the motif quilted in this same position in the quilt pictured in Plate 8.

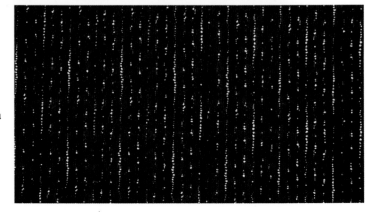

Plate 14
Diamond in the Square. Top: twill-weave wool; back: black-and-white woven-pattern cotton flannel; c. 1910. The twill-weave fabrics in muted colors suggest that this is an early twentieth century quilt.

Diamond in the Square

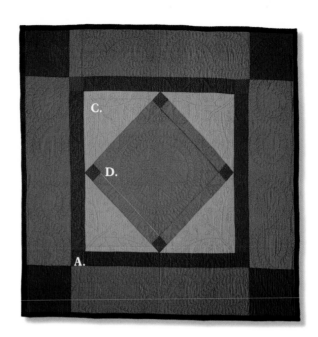

Overall dimensions: 77" square
Binding: 1.5"
Outer border: 12.25"
Inner border: 4"
Center square: 41.5"
Diamond border: 3.25"
Center diamond: 23.5"

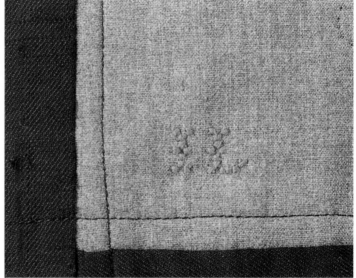

A. Detail of inner border corner block: From a distance the change from the wine inner border to the purple corner block is hardly noticeable.

B. Detail of back at corner: The initials "IL" have been cross-stitched on the back near a corner edge, using pink cotton embroidery thread. Initialing quilts in this manner was a common technique used by Lancaster County Amish women to identify either the maker or the owner of the piece.

C. The black quilting thread used throughout most Lancaster County Amish quilts shows off well here on the light green wool ground. The branching rose motif was a common, but somewhat later, quilting pattern choice for this space.

D. The glowing red twill-weave wool shows off well the fluid lines of the grapevine pattern quilting. A similar pattern, more condensed and with tighter curves to accommodate a wider dimension, is used in the narrow darker red border.

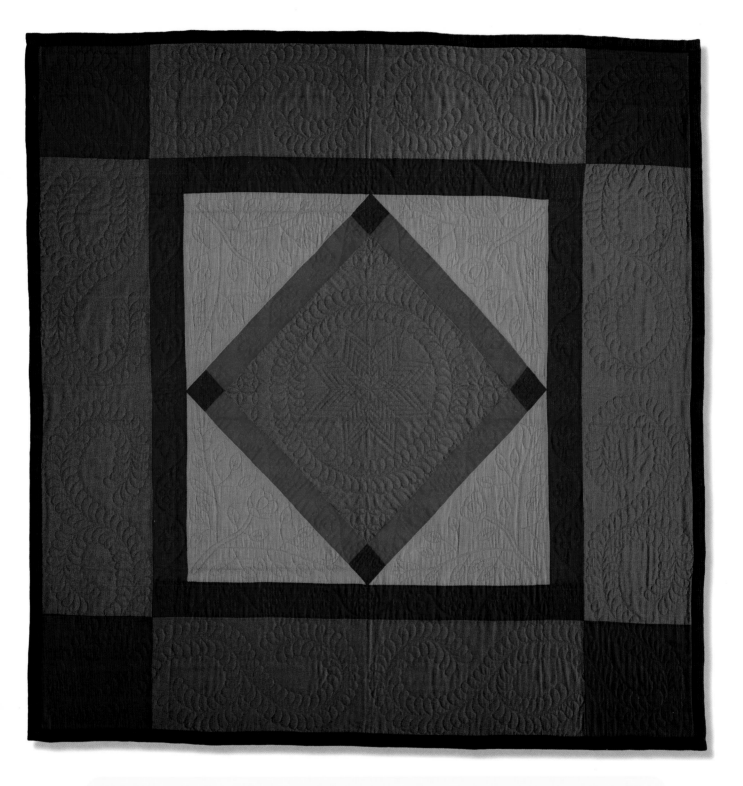

Plate 15

Diamond in the Square. Top: plain- and twill-weave wool; back: blue plain-weave cotton; initialed "IL"; c. 1925. Six shades of wool have been used to create this quilt top. The result is a lively combination of the typical Amish palate, much appreciated by today's collector. The tightly curving feather pattern adds to the robust nature of this many-colored quilt. The initials were applied by the maker or the owner. *Gift of Irene N. Walsh.*

Diamond in the Square

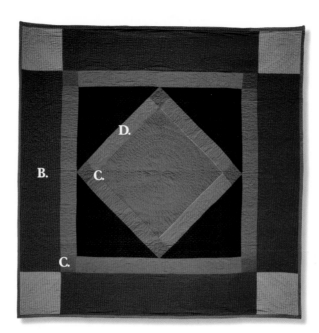

Overall dimensions: 80" square
Binding: 1"
Outer border: 11.5"
Inner border: 4.25"
Center square: 46.5"
Diamond border: 4"
Center diamond: 25.25"

A. Detail of binding and back: The hand-finished binding and plain-colored cotton backing are typical of many Lancaster County Amish quilts. But this example has the added feature of red cotton cross-stitched initials "VK" done in a manner similar to those seen on the previous quilt (Plate 15).

B. The tightly curled feather quilting in the outer border ensures that there will be little open unquilted area.

C. The quilter employed the same flower motif in all eight small green corner blocks, but in the corners of the red center diamond she placed more complex petal flowers resembling small wreaths.

D. Notice that the quilter, instead of using a grapevine in the inner diamond border, chose a meandering flower and stem design for both borders. As these two borders are similar in width, she did not have to alter her quilting pattern.

Plate 16

Diamond in the Square. Top: plain- and twill-weave wool; back: flesh-color plain-weave cotton; initialed "VK;" c. 1930. The quilter of this piece outdid the maker of the previous example (plate 15) by using six colors combined in an exceptionally pleasing way and quilted in the finest Amish style. The waffle quilting in the purple fields would suggest an earlier date than those represented by some others of this pattern. *Gift of Paul W. and Judy S. Ware.*

Diamond in the Square

Overall dimensions: 77" square
Binding: 2"
Outer border: 12.25"
Inner border: 3.5"
Center square: 41.5"
Diamond border: 3.5"
Center diamond: 21.75"

A. Detail of center diamond corner: The quilter has perhaps done her best planning in the center diamond, where there are few open spaces. The corners are neatly filled with intersecting small circles. This works well with the large central star and single feather wreath.

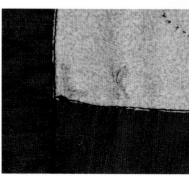

B. Detail of back: Another set of initials, "LK," is seen here in red cotton outline stitch along the back edge of the quilt. The backing material is a multicolor twill-weave cotton commonly used by Lancaster County Amish women for this purpose.

C.The maker may have chosen brown quilting thread because such a large area of the quilt is brown. The rose and tulip quilting is this area leaves large open areas even though the quilter embellished the inner borders with a scallop pattern.

Plate 17

Diamond in the Square. Top: plain- and twill-weave wool; back: multicolor twill-weave cotton; c. 1935. The more open quilting patterns in this piece suggest a slightly later date than the previous example (Plate 16). Other departures from the norm are the slightly wider binding (2-inch) and the use of brown quilting thread instead of black.

Diamond in the Square

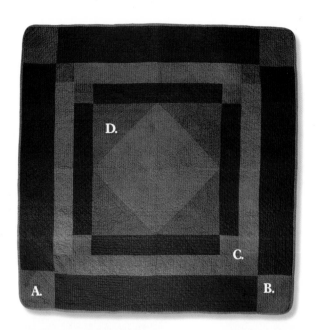

Overall dimensions: 76" square
Binding: .75"
Outer border: 9.5"
Both inner borders: 5.25"
Center square: 34.5"
Center diamond: 25"

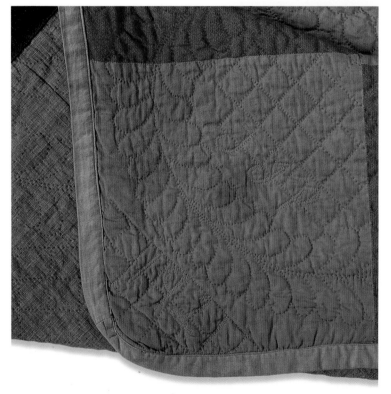

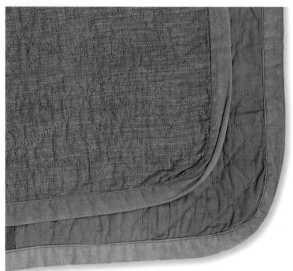

B. Detail of binding and corner: The corners are rounded and the binding is only 0.75 inch wide, while the usual Lancaster binding measures 1.5 to 2 inches. The characteristics seen here are often associated with Mifflin County, Pennsylvania, Amish quilts.

A. Detail of initials and date: The initials and date were machine-stitched into the quilt sometime after the it was taken off the quilting frame. Signed and dated Amish quilts are rare. Such examples help in dating other quilts with similar fabrics and quilting techniques.

C. Detail of first inner border and adjacent second inner border: The two equal-width narrow inner borders are a characteristic not seen in any others in this collection, but they are seen frequently in Mifflin County examples. The more circular and less linear quilting patterns in the blue inner border, accompanied by the circular pinwheels in the small corner blocks, are also Mifflin County attributes. The maroon wool fabric used in the quilt is referred to as henrietta cloth. Note the lustrous effect achieved by the interweaving of the two tones of fibers—maroon and tan

D. Detail of green triangular block: Clamshell quilting is an uncommon feature in Lancaster County Amish quilts.

Plate 18

Diamond in the Square. Top: plain-weave wool; back: blue plain-weave cotton chambray initialed and dated "JTP 1921." Significant variations from the traditional Lancaster County quilt suggest that this example may have been made in, or influenced by the traditions of, the Amish settlement in Mifflin County. Overall proportions, quilting patterns, and construction details differ somewhat from the previously pictured Diamond in the Square examples. But the Diamond in the Square pattern is usually associated with the Lancaster County Amish.

Diamond in the Square—Ninepatch variation

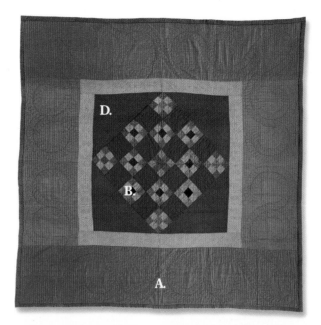

Overall dimensions: 71" square
Binding: 1.25"
Outer border: 14"
Inner border: 3.5"
Large center square: 33"
Center block: 5"

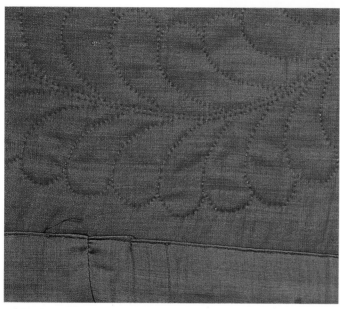

A. Detail of outer border: The red plain-weave wool material is actually woven from two different fibers and colors, red wool and white silk. Often called henrietta cloth, the fabric features an interlacing of color and fiber that produces a lovely sheen much appreciated by Amish quiltmakers.

B. Detail of Nine Patch: Note that many of the small gray and two of the mauve and orange blocks in the Nine Patch unit are pieced from even smaller sections. Perhaps the maker had only scraps of these particular fabrics.

C. Detail of back: Two cotton chambrays have been used, one woven from black-and-white and the other from blue-and-white cotton fibers.

D. The lattice pattern quilting in this green twill-weave fabric is rarely used in Lancaster County Amish quilts. A more common pattern used in this area on early quilts is the more evenly-placed lines that form the waffle pattern.

Plate 19
Diamond in the Square—Ninepatch variation. Top: plain- and twill-weave wool; back: blue-and-white and black-and-white plain-weave cotton chambray; c. 1910. Although variations of the Diamond in the Square pattern are rare, this collection includes ten unusual examples. This variation is one of the rarest and also quite early. It is also one of the smallest quilts in the collection.

Diamond in the Square—Sunshine and Shadow variation

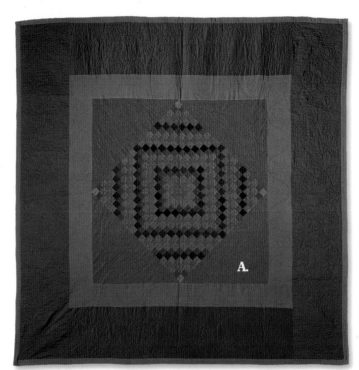

Overall dimensions: 74" square
Binding: 1.25"
Outer border: 11"
Inner border: 5"
Center square: 39.5"
Center diamond 27.5"

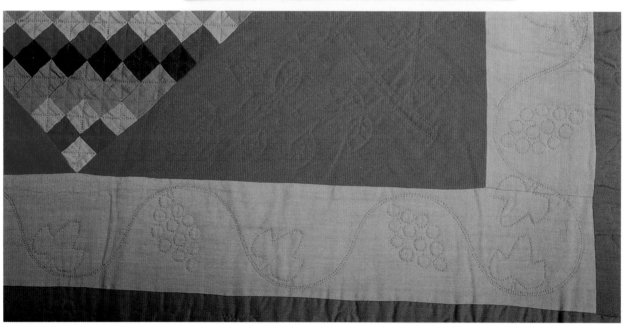

A. Detail of inner border and red triangular block: The undulating-grapevine quilting pattern leaves a large amount of empty space and suggests a later 1930s quilt, as does the branching rose motif in the red field.

B. Detail of back: A person familiar with Lancaster County Amish quilts would know, when seeing this black-and-white woven-pattern fabric backing, that it is a local Amish quilt.

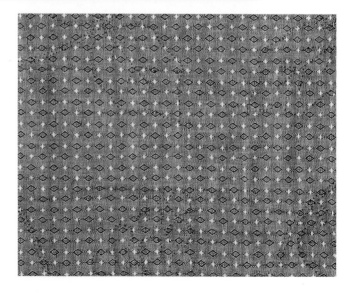

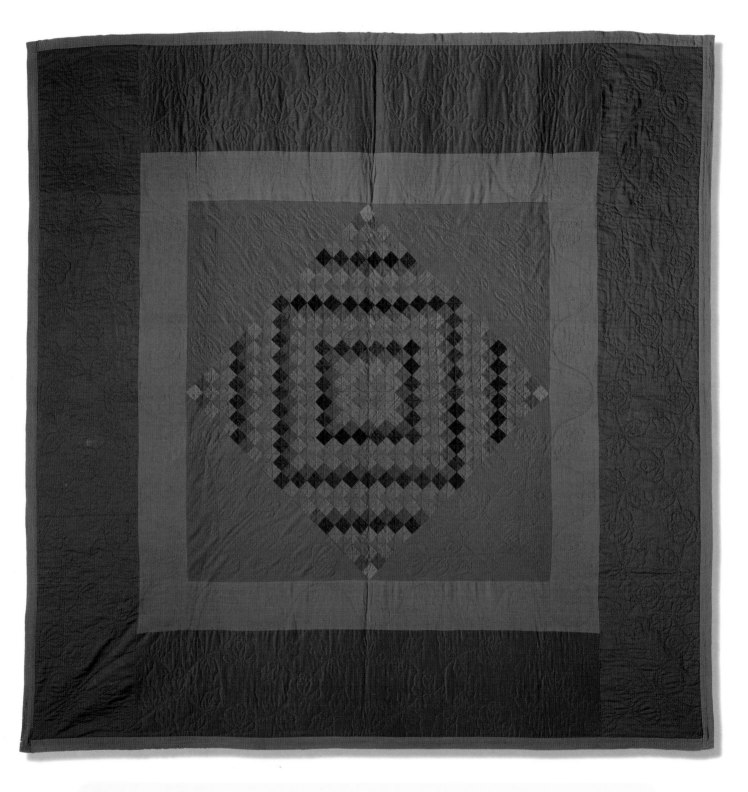

Plate 20
Diamond in the Square—Sunshine and Shadow variation. Top: plain- and twill-weave wool; back: black-and-white woven-pattern cotton; c. 1935. Of the variations on this pattern, the Sunshine and Shadow seems to be most common. This example, with regular repeating rows of color, mimics the more common overall-patterned Sunshine and Shadow quilts. *Gift of Roger Herr and Anthony Sprauve.*

Diamond in the Square—Sunshine and Shadow variation

Overall dimensions: 79" square
Binding: 1.25"
Outer border: 11"
Inner square border: 3.5"
Center square: 47.5"
Inner diamond border 2.75"
Center diamond 28.5"

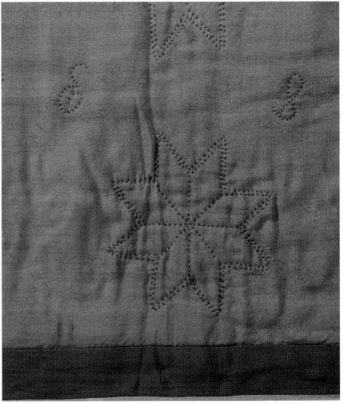

A. Detail of small block: The lines of quilting that intersect in the middle of each small block and cross from point to point are the standard block quilting pattern used by Lancaster County Amish quilters.

B. Detail of bottom middle outer border: The script initials "ES" appear on either side of the quilted star in the top border. Careful examination in this area reveals the date "1943" was once present, then was removed. This may have been done to lessen the possibility that people viewing the quilt would know the date of the quilt or would be able to calculate the maker's age. This was not an uncommon practice among sampler makers, who frequently dated their work. As women aged, they were more likely to "destroy the evidence."

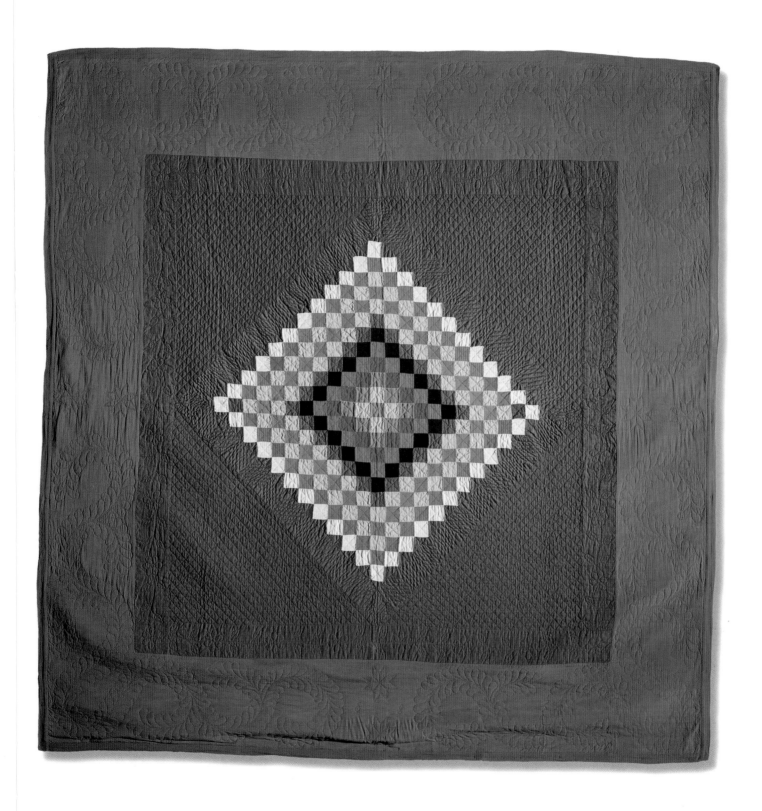

Plate 21
Diamond in the Square—Sunshine and Shadow variation. Top: plain-weave and crepe wool and rayon; back: blue plain-weave cotton; 1943. The quilting is well done and traditional for a quilt of this late date. The inclusion of rayon and crepe fabrics, together with some lighter-colored fabrics, is consistent with Amish quilting practices of the 1940s.

Diamond in the Square—Sunshine and Shadow variation

Overall dimensions: 78" square
Binding: 1.25"
Outer border: 11.5"
Inner square border: 3.5"
Center square: 45.5"
Inner diamond border: 2.5
Center diamond 28.5"

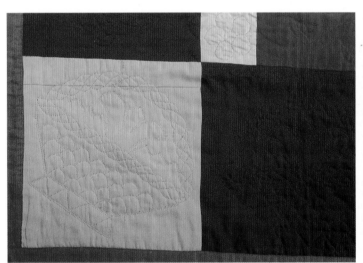

A. Detail of outer gray corner block: The handsome basket quilting used throughout the outer border is particularly noticeable in the light gray corner blocks. The braided handle and rim overflowing with fruit makes this example particularly attractive.

B. Detail of back: A handsome printed cotton fabric was chosen by the maker as backing material.

C. The same braided or cable motif found in the baskets was expanded to fill the border of the diamond center.

Plate 23
Diamond in the Square—Sunshine and Shadow variation. Top: plain- and twill-weave wool and cotton; back: blue and red plain-weave printed cotton; c. 1935. The floral quilting patterns, the variety of block colors, and the choice of wool and cotton materials in the top date this quilt in the later 1930s. *Gift of Irene N. Walsh.*

Diamond in the Square—Sunshine and Shadow variation

Overall dimensions: 80" square
Binding: 1.25"
Outer border: 13"
Inner square border: 4.5"
Center square: 42.5"
Center diamond 30"

A. Detail of outer border: The quilter created a vigorous pattern of undulating curving floral designs that fill the wide border. An added detail is the scalloping quilted along the inner edge.

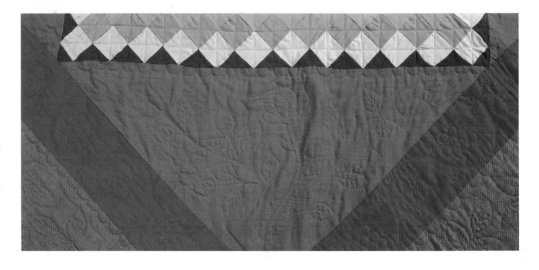

B. Detail of the inner green triangle: The branching floral designs frequently used in this area are particularly fluid and fill the space well. Again the quilter has added scalloping to the inner edge of the triangular area.

Plate 24

Diamond in the Square—Sunshine and Shadow variation. Top: purple plain- and twill-weave wool; back: purple twill-weave cotton; c. 1935. The classic colors and well-balanced arrangement of the jewel-toned fabrics fill our expectations of what most connoisseurs feel a Lancaster County Amish quilt should be. The quilt was purchased from an Amish family living in northern Lancaster County near the Leba-non County line.[3] *Gift of Great Women of Lancaster.*

Diamond in the Square—Philadelphia Pavement variation

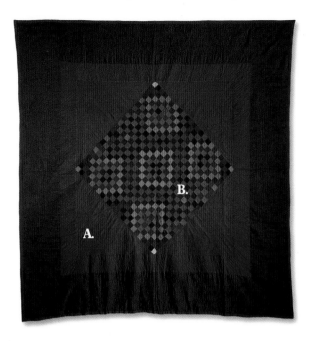

Overall dimensions: 88" square
Binding: 1"
Outer border: 12"
Inner square border: 5"
Center square: 52"
Center diamond 36"

A. Detail of the blue triangular field and inner red border: Although the outer border is quilted in an earlier feather pattern, the blue rayon crepe triangle is embellished with a later branching rose pattern. The fabric and pattern are appropriate to the late dating of this quilt. The red inner border zigzag quilting containing a four-petal flower is an unusual variation of the earlier traditional diamond and flower often used in a narrow inner border. Also notable is the heart quilted in each corner of the blue field where the point of the diamond touches the inner border. The eight hearts seem unrelated to the rest of the blue field quilting pattern.

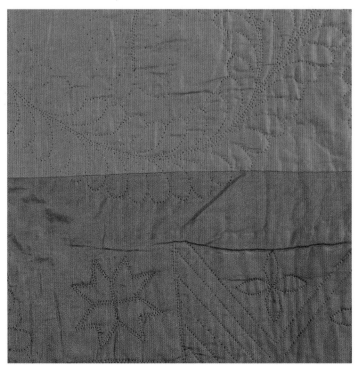

B. Detail of center of diamond block area: Close inspection reveals some imperfect piecing techniques that detract from the expected preciseness of the pattern.

C. Detail of back of quilt: The back has been pieced from a selection of several green fabrics; the lighter green piece is wool and the darker fabric is cotton.

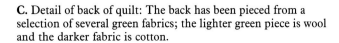

Plate 25

Diamond in the Square—Philadelphia Pavement variation. Top: plain- and twill-weave and crepe wool and rayon; back: green pieced plain- and sateen-weave cotton and wool; c. 1935. The maker of this quilt, Fanny Petersheim (1879-1941), probably produced it near the end of her life, as the rayon fabrics it incorporates were not commonly used by the Lancaster County Amish until the later 1930s.[4] The large size of the quilt also suggests a later date. There are no corner blocks used in the piece, but the unusual arrangement of the small blocks within the center diamond adds plenty of visual excitement. The quilt is an interesting combination of an older traditional pattern and a new innovative block arrangement as a center motif.

Diamond in the Square—Sunshine and Shadow variation

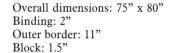

Overall dimensions: 75" x 80"
Binding: 2"
Outer border: 11"
Block: 1.5"
Center diamond 21.5"

A. Detail of corner of outer border: The corner lyre pattern, as well as the accompanying fat feather or fern fronds around the edges, is unusual and suggests an early 1900s date. The choice of cotton in the top is not common for this period of time.

B. Detail of basket quilting in the center diamond points: The small basket motif quilted in each point of the pink center diamond is exquisite and matches in interest and quality the unusual star and four-petal flower pattern in the center. One can infer from the lack of alignment of the inner border of black blocks that the piecing gave the maker a bit more trouble than the quilting.

C. Detail of back: The appearance of a check pattern is created by brown printing on white cotton cloth. This type of cotton fabric was popular with Lancaster County Amish quilters.

Plate 26

Diamond in the Square—Sunshine and Shadow variation. Top: plain- and twill-weave and sateen wool and cotton; back: brown-and-white check-print, plain-weave cotton; c. 1910. Although this pattern could have been formatted as a square quilt, the maker chose to make it as a rectangle. The pattern is an unusual combination of Diamond in the Square and Sunshine and Shadow patterns. It reverses the location of the blocks from that arrangement seen in the previous variations of this pattern. Equally interesting are the unusual quilting patterns employed by this innovative maker.

Diamond in the Square—Nine Patch and Sawtooth variation

Overall dimensions: 73.5" square
Binding: 1"
Outer border: 13.5"
Inner square border: 4.75"
Center square: 35
Diamond border: 2"
Center diamond 21.5"

A. Detail of back: The backing material is a black-and-white cotton chambray, a popular choice among Lancaster Amish quilts, but unlikely to be used in clothing because of its slight pattern, derived from the weave structure.

B. The quilting in the outer border of baskets, stars, and flower devices is bold but not heavily quilted.

C. The same boldness continues with the cable quilting in the almost-orange inner border and the lattice quilting in the inner gray triangles. These patterns are not commonly used in Lancaster County Amish quilts.

Plate 27

Diamond in the Square—Nine Patch and Sawtooth variation. Top: plain- and twill-weave and crepe wool; back: black-and-white cotton chambray; c. 1927. Katie Stoltzfus was the maker of this unusual, and perhaps unique, quilt.[5] The elements of the classic Center Diamond pattern have been strikingly altered with the addition of an unexpected combination of smaller patterns in the central block. *Gift of Irene N. Walsh.*

Diamond in the Square—Sunshine and Shadow variation

Overall dimensions: 76" square
Binding: 1.25"
Outer border: 12.5"
Diamond border: 6"
Block: 2"

A. Detail of top center of outer border: The wide space in the outer border has been filled by the quilter with fat curving feather motifs and a large round flower as an additional fill-in motif. In this area the quilter did not have quite enough room to finish her feather.

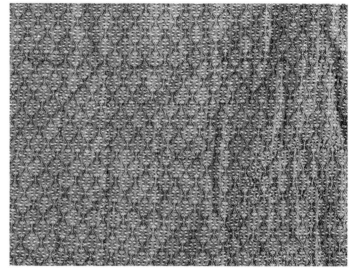

C. Detail of back: The black-and-white woven-cotton patterned material is a classic choice for quilt backing in Lancaster County Amish quilts. One could identify this as Lancaster Amish quilt by seeing only the backing fabric and its wide applied wool binding.

B. Detail of the inner green border: The unusually wide border also has been filled with robust curving patterns. The quilter chose grapevines and filled the area using large leaves, grapes, and almost semicircular curving vines.

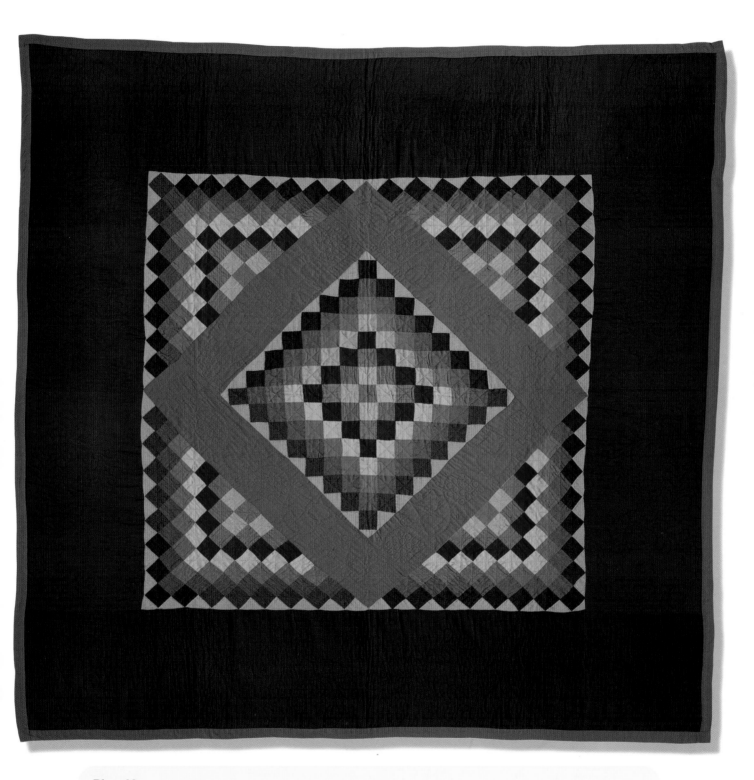

Plate 28
Diamond in the Square—Sunshine and Shadow variation. Top: plain- and twill-weave, and crepe wool and rayon; back: black-and-white woven-pattern cotton; c. 1935. The maker of this quilt used two traditional Lancaster patterns, in a way that makes its pattern just a step outside the usual boundaries. The insertion of a wide green diamond border and the selection of surrounding bright blocks on each side of the diamond add visual excitement in an innovative way. *Gift of Charles and Molly Milner.*

Sunshine and Shadow

Overall dimensions: 79.25" square
Binding: 1.25"
Outer border: 11"
Inner border: 3.75"
Block: 1.75"

A. Detail of block: Close examination reveals the wide variety of plain- and twill-weave and crepe wool and silk fabrics used in this example.

B. Detail of back: This black-and-white woven-pattern cotton fabric is another example of the many similar cotton fabrics commonly used as backing by the Lancaster County Amish community.

Plate 29

Sunshine and Shadow. Top: plain- and twill-weave, and crepe wool and silk; back: black-and-white woven-pattern cotton; c. 1930. This is a classic Sunshine and Shadow design, but the palate is lighter than in most Lancaster Sunshine and Shadow quilts. The quilting patterns in the outer and inner borders are frequently seen in quilts made before 1930. Light fabric blocks alternate with the dark suggesting the descriptive pattern name. This quilt and the one seen next (Plate 30) have the same block size, general layout, and border measurements. But because of color choice and manipulation their appearance is quite dissimilar.

Sunshine and Shadow

A.

Overall dimensions: 79.25"
square
Binding: 1.25"
Outer border: 11"
Inner border: 3.75"
Block: 1.75"

A. Detail of outer and inner border: The tightly curved feather-pattern quilting provides dense coverage of the outer border and can be considered one of the classic patterns used in fine Lancaster County Amish quilts. The grapevine quilting in the narrow green inner border mirrors the fine quality of quilting seen in the outer border.

Plate 30
Sunshine and Shadow. Top: twill- and plain-weave wool; back: dark blue satin-weave polished cotton; c. 1930. The maker of this quilt chose dark jewel-like tones, highlighted with bright pink "sunshine" rows. She combined these colors with extraordinary quilting to make a memorable work of art.

Sunshine and Shadow

A.

Overall dimensions: 80" square
Binding: 1.25"
Outer border: 10.5"
Inner border: 3.75"
Block: 2.125"

A. Detail of outer and inner borders: In this quilt all the border quilting patterns are leaf and floral vines. The only geometric quilting present is the intersecting line pattern running throughout the small center blocks. This is the traditional method of quilting small block patterns in Lancaster County Amish quilts. Intertwining leaf and floral vines fill the dark outer border. The maker also added scalloping at the inner edge. Related floral vine motifs are stretched out to appropriately fill this narrow space of the inner border.

Plate 31
Sunshine and Shadow. Top: plain- and twill-weave wool; back: purple sateen-weave cotton; c. 1930.
The coordination of colors between the outer borders and the Sunshine and Shadow blocks helps the
eye focus on the play of colors in the center square. There the colors seem to group in bands of three,
adding to the liveliness of the pattern.

Sunshine and Shadow

Overall dimensions: 78" square
Binding: 1"
Outer border: 10.5"
Inner border: 4"
Block: 1.625"

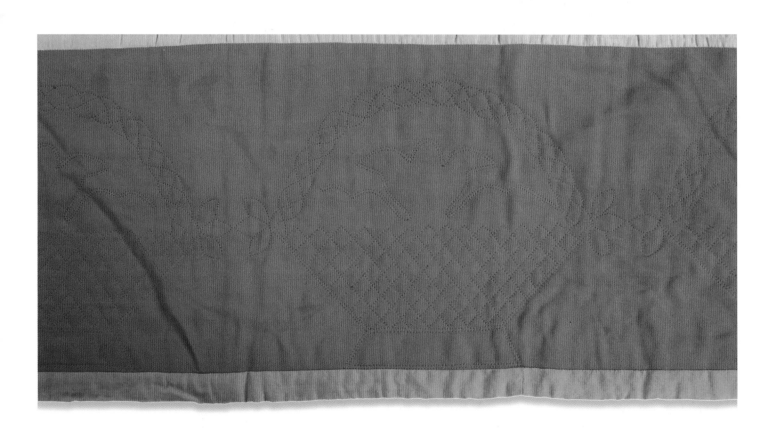

A. Detail of outer back border: The basket motifs, quilted with dark thread, are well designed and executed, but don't stand out as strongly as the lighter pink quilting thread. This area, like the other non-pink areas is quilted with the traditional black thread.

B. The use of pink as quilting thread to blend with the pink areas of the quilt was an unusual choice for a Lancaster County Amish quilter to make. Note too that the corner blocks are quilted with a motif different from those found in the rest of the outer border. These floral motifs seem unrelated to the basket quilting along the sides.

C. Notice the use of two white blocks in place of the lavender blocks. White is not a commonly used color in Lancaster County Amish quilts.

Plate 32

Sunshine and Shadow. Top: plain-weave rayon, cotton, and wool; back: blue-and-white woven-check plain-weave cotton; c. 1940. The predominant use of cotton and rayon over wool in this quilt suggests a date close to 1940, when fine woolen fabrics previously used in Lancaster County Amish quilts were becoming less available in the marketplace. Notice the use of red pink and maroon in adjacent blocks. "English" (i.e., non-Amish) quilt makers of the period would hardly have chosen such a palate.

Overall dimensions: 85" square
Binding: 1.5"
Outer border: 10.25"
Inner border: 3.75"
Block: 2"

A. Detail of outer border: The quilting patterns are similar to those used in the previous quilt. The corner block is the same floral device, but the baskets are less intricately quilted. There is an additional scalloping added to the inner edge of the border to fill in the open area. This quilt contains a darker spectrum of colors than the one seen in Plate 32.

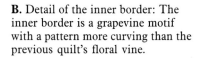

B. Detail of the inner border: The inner border is a grapevine motif with a pattern more curving than the previous quilt's floral vine.

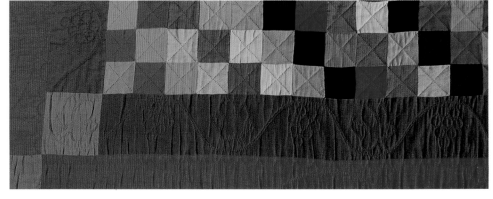

Plate 33

Sunshine and Shadow. Top: plain- and twill-weave and crepe wool; back: green plain-weave cotton; c. 1927. Arie Esh made this quilt for her son Daniel before his marriage in 1928.[6] The common practice in Amish homes is to make sure that all of the children have quilts to take to their new homes. Depending upon family members' quilting abilities and time, there may be several produced for each child, including boys.

Sunshine and Shadow

Overall dimensions: 82.25" square
Binding: 1.625"
Outer border: 12"
Inner border: 4.25"
Block: 1.5"

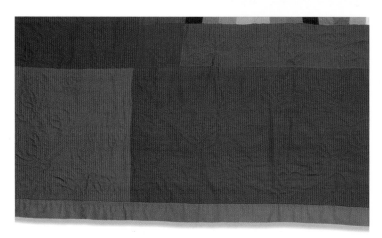

A. Detail of outer border: The open curving rose pattern is a later development and also suggests that this quilt was made about 1940.

C. Detail of the back: The backing fabric is one of the wilder examples seen in this collection. The palate, however, is still within the color limits of the Lancaster County Amish community.

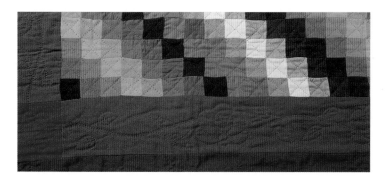

B. Detail of inner border: The large rose pattern quilted in this area does not need to curve to fill the space. This comparatively straight effect gives a stiffer appearance to the design.

Plate 34

Sunshine and Shadow. Top: plain- and twill-weave wool, cotton, and rayon; back: brown, pink, and white printed, plain-weave cotton; c. 1940. Although the colors in this example are deep and glowing, as seen in many earlier Lancaster County Amish quilts, the inclusion of many cotton and rayon fabrics suggests that it was made later in the century. *Gift of Irene N. Walsh.*

Sunshine and Shadow

Overall dimensions: 81" square
Binding: 1.25"
Outer border: 10.5"
Inner border: 4.25"
Block: 2.125"

A. Detail of back: The dark blue striped cotton sateen is an elegant, rather reserved choice for the back of this quilt.

B. It is not common to see such a large-scale and open diamond and four-petal design used within the narrow inner border.

Plate 35
Sunshine and Shadow. Top: plain-weave, twill-weave, and crepe wool and rayon; back: dark blue woven-stripe sateen-weave cotton; c. 1940. The large center blocks and contrasting colors give this quilt a bold, almost garish appearance. Non-Amish quilters would not likely have chosen these startling color arrangements, which shade from crimson to orange to pink.

Sunshine and Shadow

Overall dimensions: 78" square
Binding: 1.25"
Outer border: 12"
Inner triple border: 3.75"
Corner block: 5.5" square
Block: 1.75"

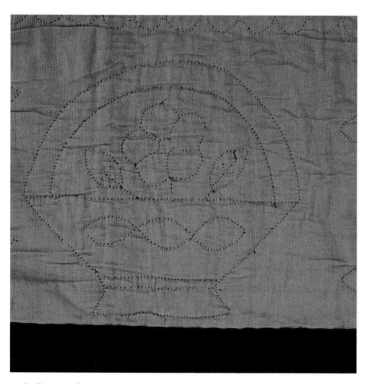

A. Detail of outer border from back: Even the quilting patterns vary from the norm. The rather open basket and floral motif, seen here from the back of the quilt, differs from others previously seen.

B. Detail of inner triple border and corner block: Quilting patterns have been altered to fit the changed proportions of the inner borders of this quilt.

C. The corner block star quilting motif seems unrelated to the rest of the border.

Plate 36
Sunshine and Shadow. Top: plain-weave, twill-weave, and crepe wool; back: tan plain-weave cotton; c. 1940. The maker of this quilt was adventuresome enough to experiment with her inner border design. A pieced border made up of three narrow strips is anchored with large corner blocks. *Gift of Sarah H. Slaymaker.*

Sunshine and Shadow

Overall dimensions: 80" square
Binding: 1.75"
Outer border: 10.5"
Inner border: 4.5"
Inner border strips: 1.5"
Block: 1.5"

A. Detail of outer border, center bottom: The two-tone silk and wool henrietta cloth used in this quilt top, along with the fern quilting motif, suggests that this quilt was made in the early 1900s. The maker chose to insert her initials "JE," in the quilting at this central area of the outer border.

B. The simple cable quilting is not a common pattern used in narrow inner borders but seems appropriate to the early date of this piece.

Plate 37
Sunshine and Shadow. Top: plain-weave, twill-weave, and henrietta wool and silk; back: black-and-white printed polka dot plain-weave cotton; c. 1910. There is a small body of Sunshine and Shadow quilts containing these unusual segmented inner borders. It is likely they were made by either family members or close friends. Signed in the quilting: "JE."

Overall dimensions: 74.5" square
Binding: 1"
Outer border: 13"
Inner border: 3.25"
Center red and green strips: 5.5"
Outside green strips: 6.25"

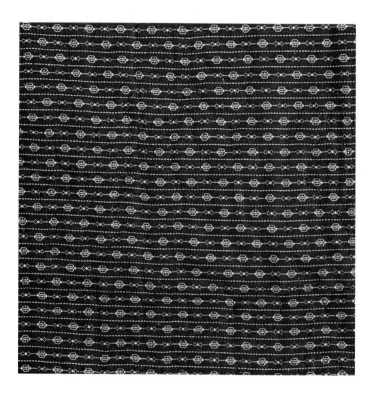

A. Detail of back: The delightful woven-patterned blue-and-white cotton is too handsome to remain unseen on the back of this quilt. These small patterned cottons were often the choice of Amish quilters for use as backing material. Most frequently they were of blue-and-white or black-and-white combinations.

B. The dark quilting stands out on this unusually light pink inner border. Although there is little contrast, the maker did add corner blocks to the inner border of her quilt. The rose pattern is consistent with a quilt of this date.

Plate 43

Bars. Top: plain-weave wool and cotton; back: blue-and-white woven-patterned plain-weave cotton; c. 1940. Compare this bright-colored quilt with the previous Bars quilt (Plate 42), made from strong darker colors. Because of its color and quilting patterns, this piece can be dated at least twenty years later. It is square, a less common shape for the Bars pattern. A subtle motion has been put into play by the maker's use of varied bar widths.

Overall dimensions: 74" x 82"
Binding: 1.75"
Outer border: 11"
Inner border: 3.25"
Strips: 6"

A. Detail of inner border: The typical four-petal flower within triangular lines, quilted with dark thread, blends into the deep blue color of the inner border.

B. Detail of back: The tan printed fabric gives a subtle yet interesting appearance to the back of the quilt.

C. The quilter has isolated her corner blocks with color and a stand-alone feather-wreath quilting pattern. Note the segmented feather pattern used in the rest of the outer border. It is an unusual variation of the traditional continuous feather pattern and stands out well on the light tan fabric. The binding on this quilt, measuring 1.75 inches, is slightly wider than on most Lancaster County Amish examples.

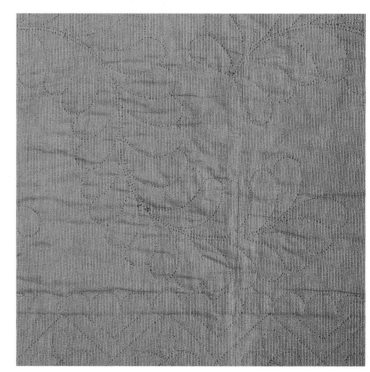

Plate 44

Bars. Top: twill-weave wool; back: brown-and-tan printed-stripe plain-weave cotton; c. 1925. This Bars pattern contains inner and outer corner blocks with a pleasing progression of red fabric from the outer corner to the central part of the quilt. The contrast of light and dark adds to the visual appeal.

Overall dimensions: 72.5" x 81"
Binding: 1.25"
Outer border: 10.5"
Inner border: 3.25"
Strips: 6"

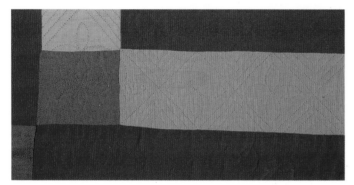

A. Detail of inner border and corner block: The finer quilting patterns suggest this quilt was made earlier than the previous example.

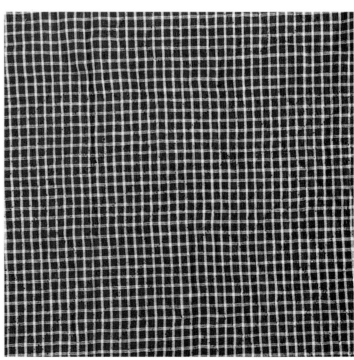

B. Detail of the back: The blue-and-white cotton woven-check pattern adds a crisp look to the back surface.

Plate 45

Bars. Top: plain-weave wool; back: blue-and-white woven-check plain-weave cotton; c. 1920. This quilt, although quite different in color, is remarkably similar in pattern layout, dimensions, and quilting to the previous quilt (Plate 44). Notice particularly the outside border with the unusual segmented feather pattern quilting and the stand-alone feather wreath in each corner block. The waffle quilting in the central portion of this quilt and its inner border quilting are tighter than in the example shown in the previous plate. The liberal use of strong red against teal, accented with a narrow pink border, adds excitement to this bedcover.

Overall dimensions: 77.5" square
Binding: 1.25"
Outer border: 10.5"
Inner border: 4.5"
Strips: 5"

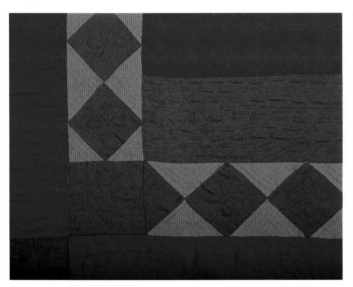

A. Detail of inner border at corner: Although the maker was unable to use full blocks all around the inner border, halving the deep green against the dark blue corner blocks resolves this problem without distraction. The seven-petal flower quilted in the corner block is well executed and of a larger scale than the four-petal bloom repeated in the borders. The quilting in the corner block, the outer-border continuous feather, and the center-area waffle quilting are consistent with a 1920s date.

B. Detail of back: The handsome check print serves as backing material. The brown-and-white color is less frequently seen than the blue-and-white or black-and-white combination.

Plate 46

Bars. Top: plain-weave wool; back: brown-and-white printed-check plain-weave cotton; c. 1925. The four-petal flower within a diamond quilting pattern, frequently used by Lancaster County Amish quilters to fill the inner borders, has been converted by this maker into an actual pieced diamond pattern. The quilting pattern is now secondary to the piecing. Although this interesting variation appears in two quilts in the collection, Plates 46 and 47, examples such as these are rare. This quilt contains nine bars in the center section, as does the quilt seen in Plate 39, instead of the more common seven strips. *Gift in memory of Louise Stoltzfus.*

Split Bars

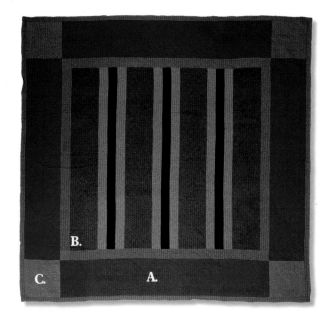

Overall dimensions: 76" x 80.5"
Binding: 1.5"
Outer border: 10"
Inner border: 2.5"
Green strips: 7.5"
Narrow strips: 2.5"

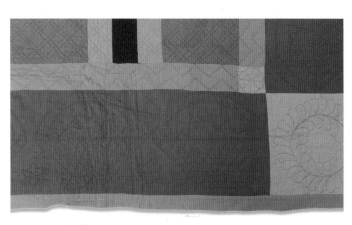

A. Detail of outer border: Simple but well-planned baskets and stars fill the border.

B. Detail of inner border and center quilting: The double zigzag pattern was not commonly used in Lancaster County Amish quilts, nor does one usually see center area lattice quilting. All the quilting is well executed.

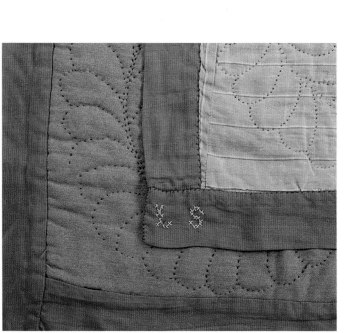

C. Detail of corner, back and initials: The cross-stitched initials are worked with white cotton right on the binding and may identify the owner or maker. Even the backing fabric is slightly different from most used in Lancaster County Amish quilts.

Plate 48
Split Bars. Top: plain-weave wool; back: blue-green printed stripe, plain-weave cotton; c. 1930. With this variant of the Bars pattern alternating inner strips are split into three sections. The quilting patterns vary in interesting ways from the usual patterns but are all well placed and balanced. The letters "LS" have been cross-stitched on the back binding.

Split Bars

Overall dimensions: 77" x 80"
Binding: 1.25"
Outer border: 10.25"
Inner border: 3.75"
Blue strips: 6.5"
Narrow strips: 2.25"

B.

A. Detail of back: The multicolor print of the backing fabric simulates a woven structure. It adds interest without calling undue attention to itself.

B. The baskets are more closely quilted in this example than in the one shown in Plate 48. Although there are no stars to fill open space, the quilter has added a row of scalloping to the interior border. Even the majority of variations in design chosen by Lancaster County Amish quilters fall within a certain well-defined boundary of consistency and that is true here.

Plate 49

Split Bars. Top: plain- and twill-weave wool; back: multicolor printed plain-weave cotton; c. 1925. This Split Bars variation differs from the example in Plate 48 in both proportion and the placement of the bars, giving it the appearance of a more complex pattern.

Split Bars

Overall dimensions: 77" x 78"
Binding: 1.75"
Outer border: 8.25"
Inner border: 4.5"
Red strips: 4.25"
Narrow strips: 1.5"

A. Detail of inner border and corner block: Within the constraints of the small (4.25 inch square) corner block, the quilter managed to squeeze in a robust bunch of grapes. The grapevine quilting pattern that complements the corner grape bunches was well designed and placed within the triple-strip inner border.

Plate 50

Split Bars. Top: Plain- and twill-weave wools; back; tan plain-weave cotton; c. 1930. The maker of this quilt innovatively introduced the split bar configuration to create the inner border. Although this appears to be a simple design approach, it is rarely seen in Lancaster Bars quilts.

Split Bars

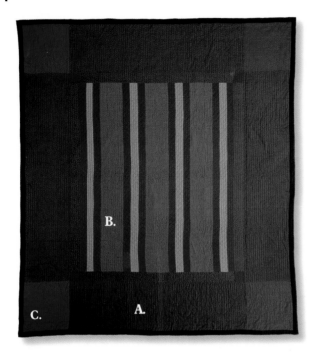

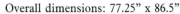
Overall dimensions: 77.25" x 86.5"
Binding: 1.5"
Outer border: 13"
Inner border: 2.75"
Green strips: 6.25"
Narrow strips: 2"

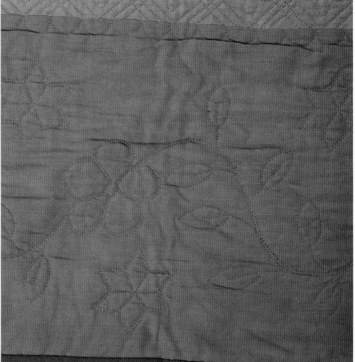

A. Detail of outer border: Wide curving floral vines fill the outer border with the addition of an inner scalloped edge and stars that echo the stars found in the broad green bar quilting.

B. Detail of inner bar section: The split bar section is waffle-quilted, and the single wide green strip contains an interesting flower vine with added stars.

C. Detail of binding: On close inspection the hand-finished binding of this quilt appears to be a later replacement. The material is a later green plain-weave wool

Plate 51

Split Bars. Top: plain-weave wool; back: brown-and-black printed-check, plain-weave cotton; c. 1935. The center block contains an unusual style of quilting also seen in the Bars quilt pictured in Plate 52. Instead of the traditional overall waffle or lattice-pattern quilting, various strip segments are treated individually.

Split Bars

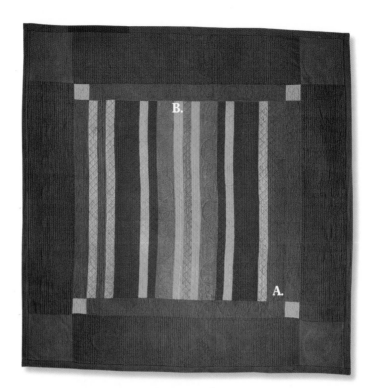

Overall dimensions: 76"
square
Binding: 1.5"
Outer border: 10.5"
Inner border: 3.5"
Wide strips: 3.75"
Narrow strips: 2"

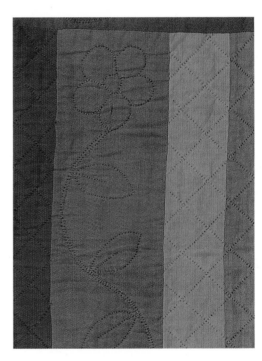

A. Detail of inner border: With slight variation to accommodate the width of the strip, the floral vine motif is repeated in the inner border and in the inner wide strips.

B. Detail of wide strip and adjacent narrow red strip: Note the similarity of this floral vine to the inner border quilting. The uninhibited way in which Amish women combined various shades of red and pink probably surprised their more color-coordinated "English" neighbors.

Plate 52

Split Bars. Top: plain-weave and crepe wool; back: black-and-white twill printed-pattern plain-weave cotton; c. 1935. The slight asymmetry within the center square is unexpected but not displeasing. It is impossible to know if this was purposeful or resulting from a shortage of the lavender fabric. Another break with tradition is the quilting of the broad strips with a floral pattern, similar to the method used in the previous quilt (Plate 51). Both of these variations are unusual in a Lancaster County Amish quilt. This quilt is one of the few square Bars patterns in the collection.

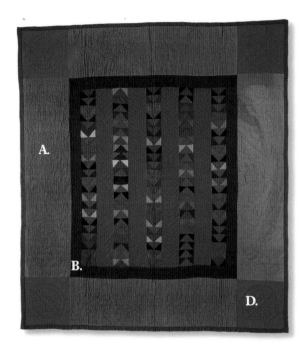

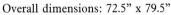

Overall dimensions: 72.5" x 79.5"
Binding: 1.25"
Outer border: 12.5"
Inner border: 3"
Wide strips: 4.75"
Pieced strips: 4"

A. Detail of outer border: The fern motif as a quilting pattern is associated with late nineteenth or early twentieth century Amish quilts, yet the use of a crepe weave wool in the binding suggests that the quilt was made as late as the 1920s.

B. Detail of the inner border at corner and wide red central strip: Note that the cable stitching in the narrow inner border does not turn the corner. The chevron quilting pattern complements the triangular Wild Goose Chase pieced work but is not usually seen in the bar section of Lancaster County Amish quilts.

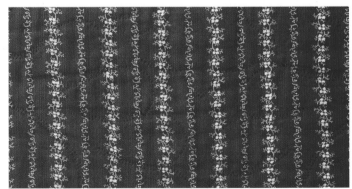

C. Detail of back: The backing fabric is shown here as an example of one of the many pleasant choices of printed cottons chosen by the Lancaster County Amish. It provideds a lively addition of color to the quilt

D. The corner basket motif suggests a slightly later date than the fern pattern seen in the rest of the outer border.

Plate 53

Bars—Wild Goose Chase variation. Top: Plain-weave and crepe wool; back: wine-and-white floral-print, plain-weave cotton; c. 1920. The Bars pattern is a common Lancaster County Amish tradition, but incorporating the Wild Goose Chase is rare, if not unique. The quilting patterns used also are unexpected. *Gift of Irene N. Walsh.*

Bars—Segmented variation

Overall dimensions: 62.25" x 75"
Binding: 1"
Outer border: 10"
Strips: 5.75"

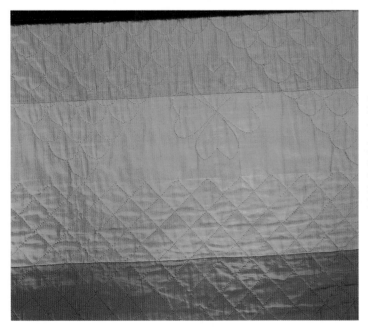

A. Detail of back: The back is made from multiple pieces of material, not a common type of backing for a Lancaster County Amish quilt.

B. An interesting outer border quilting pattern consists of a large scale four-heart motif, triangular groupings of clam shells, and one isolated feather strip in each bottom corner. The central area features the more traditional waffle quilting. All the quilting patterns are of a larger scale than usual.

Plate 54

Bars—Segmented variation. Top: twill-weave wools; back: pieced brown-and-tan plain-weave cotton; c.1910. This example is even more of a departure from the expected Lancaster County Amish Bar pattern than the previous Wild Goose Chase variation (Plate 53). Although it is bordered on only three sides, which is not an uncommon variation, the absence of an inner border results in less definition of the center field. The pattern is suggestive of a quilt made in an Amish community in the Midwest. Perhaps there was intermarriage between members of the Lancaster County Amish and a western Amish community that influenced the making of this piece. The placement of the color segments does not add to the orderliness and balance one is used to seeing in Lancaster County Amish quilts.

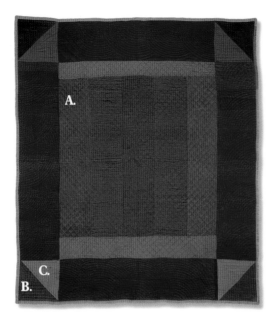

Overall dimensions: 76" x 86"
Binding: 1"
Outer border: 12"
Top inner border: 6.5"
Bottom inner border: 4.75"
Center strips: 10"

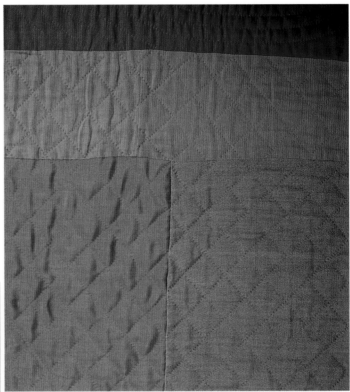

A. Details of brown outer strip: The two brown strips in the center part of the quilt, as well as the matching brown bottom inner triangles of the corner blocks, were replaced at a later date with hand-piecing. Apparently the fabric originally used did not stand up over time.

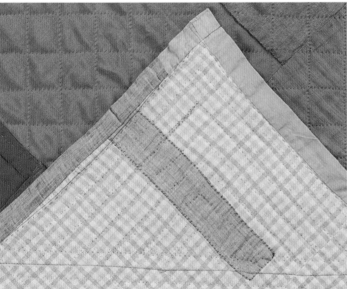

B. Detail of bottom corner block from the back: The later addition of machine stitching can be seen here against the interesting brown-and-white printed-check cotton backing. This supports the idea that the two bottom corner block brown inner corner triangles were replaced at a later date. Also present is a small gray strip applied to the backing material. The same gray material was inserted in the original orange binding and appears to be a replacement.

C. Detail of corner block and replaced binding from the front: The dark brown material was pieced in by hand and the new binding was machine stitched in place.

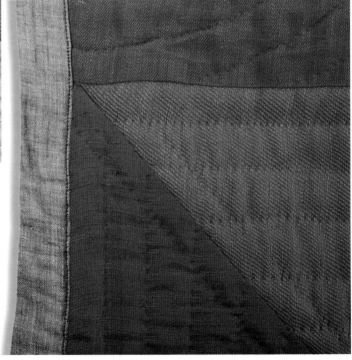

Plate 55

Bars. Top: Plain- and twill-weave wool; back: brown-and-white printed-check plain-weave cotton; c. 1880. This quilt has been placed at the end of the Bars section because it does not relate to other, more traditional Lancaster County examples known to the collecting community. As with the Bars pattern pictured in Plate 54, this pattern may be the result of some mixing of various Amish community cultures. It appears to be one of the earliest quilts in the collection. The large scale of the pattern and diagonally divided corner blocks do not fit within the usual parameters. Although the fan pattern of quilting in the outer border is unusual, it is not unique and can be seen in the quilts shown in Plates 56 and 66.

Ninepatch variation

Overall dimensions: 77.5" square
Binding: 1"
Outer border: 9"
Sashing: 3.5"
Large block: 10" square

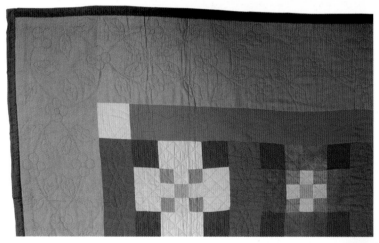

A. Detail outer and inner border at the top corner: Floral vine quilting, found in many of the later quilts, fills the outer dark blue border. The cable pattern is a less common motif in Lancaster County quilts but adapts well as an inner border and sashing motif. Note how well the pattern intersects at each junction, and observe the interesting solution the quilter uses to negotiate the inner border corners.

B. Detail of back: Cotton chambray, a material frequently used as backing for Lancaster County Amish quilts, is seen here in a pleasing wine-and-white combination.

Plate 57

Ninepatch variation. Top: plain-weave, twill-weave, and crepe wool; binding: sateen-weave cotton; back; wine-and-white cotton chambray; c. 1940. The maker designed an interesting and well-balanced quilt. Each unit or block consists of a Ninepatch block surrounded by more blockwork to form a larger, but not symmetrical, Ninepatch block. Four matching lighter center blocks draw the eye to a focal point. The four corner blocks constitute another matching group and the remaining blocks are of a third type. Some visual orientation is also provided by the one brown narrow inner border at the top of the quilt.

Ninepatch variation

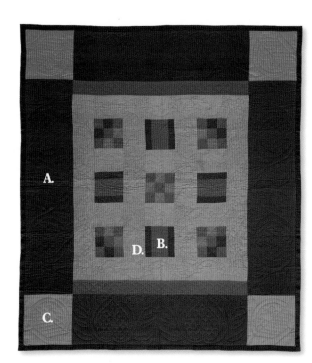

Overall dimensions: 65.25" x 71.34"
Binding: 1.25"
Outer border: 11.25"
Inner border: 3.25"
Inner sashing: 5"
Ninepatch block: 2.25"
Threepatch block: 1.5" and 3.75"

A. Detail of outer border quilting: A truly beautiful innovative pattern is used in the outer green border. Large hearts filled with clamshell quilting alternate with fern-like leaves. An added scalloped edge and graceful individual leaves fill in the open areas.

B. Detail of Threepatch block: What a surprise to see large tulips quilted in each of these four blocks!

C. The bright raspberry corner blocks are filled with lovely basket quilting and a wandering leaf from the green border.

D. The light-colored field is innovatively filled with closely quilted floral vines, a design seen frequently in longitudinal configurations in other quilts in the collection.

Plate 58

Ninepatch variation. Top: plain- and twill-weave wool; back: blue-and-white cotton chambray; c. 1920. This quilt, made by a member of the Zook family,[10] combines an unusual pattern with some classic and also rare quilting forms. The result is perhaps a unique form for a Lancaster County Amish quilt. Although the inner border appears on only two sides instead of the usual four, it in no way detracts from the overall design. Attention is drawn to the interesting combination of Ninepatch and Threepatch center blocks.

"H" Quilt

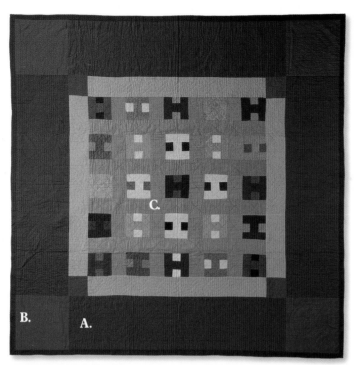

Overall dimensions: 77.25" square
Binding: 1.5"
Outer border: 12.5"
Inner border: 4.5"
Sashing: 3.5"
Small block: 1.75"

A. Detail of outer border. The fern pattern and accompanying large-scale scalloped edging is well designed and executed. This motif is less commonly used than the feather or floral vine borders.

B. The basket design shows up well against the bright red and reveals interesting variations from the usual. This is obviously a flower basket, but the detail on the front of the basket is a variation not seen on other quilts in the collection.

C. The simple quilted intersecting curves satisfy the need to quilt the area without complication.

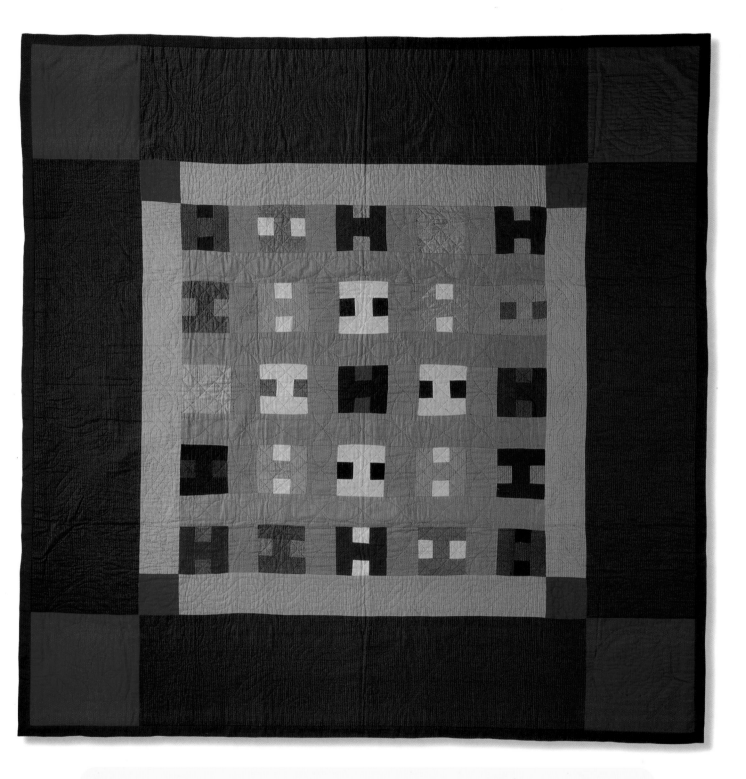

Plate 59

"H" Quilt; Top: plain- and twill-weave cotton and wool; back: purple plain-weave cotton; c. 1940. "English" quilters occasionally chose quilt patterns using a significant family initial. Because this practice is otherwise unknown within the Lancaster County Amish community, the maker of this piece may have just liked the configuration and not thought of it as an alphabet pattern.

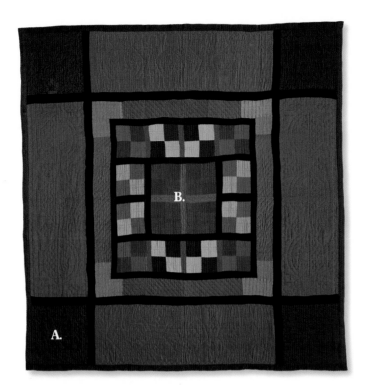

Overall dimensions: 74.25" square
Binding: 1.5"
Outer border: 13"
Inner narrow black border: 1.75"
Inner blue border: 3.75"
Inner sashing: 1.25"
Single Fourblock: 3.5" square

A. Detail of outer corner block: The quilting in the large corner block is quite different from the traditional basket design along the rest of the wide border.

B. Detail of Fourpatch and sashing: This innovative design calls for a departure from the usual Lancaster County quilting patterns. Simpler more open quilting is used throughout the center areas of the quilt.

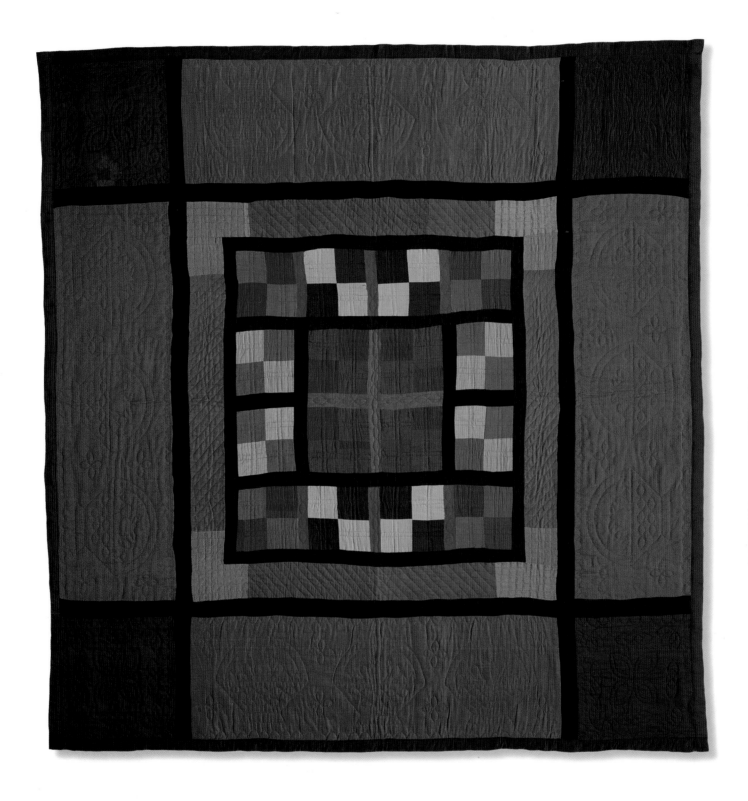

Plate 60
Fourpatch. Top: plain-, twill-weave, and crepe wool; back: black-and-white cotton chambray; c. 1935.
Although the general format, the colored wool fabrics, and the basket quilting patterns are typical of
Lancaster County Amish quilts, this maker added her personal innovations to create an unusual Fourpatch
design.

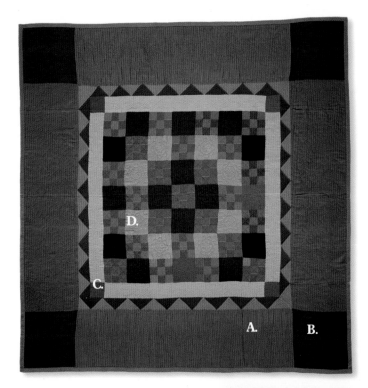

Overall dimensions: 80.5" square
Binding: 1.25"
Outer border: 13.5"
Inner diamond border: 2.5"
Inner pink border: 3.5"
Center open block: 5.625" square
Small block: 1.875" square

A. Detail of outside border: A continuous undulating feather motif, with no branching, was quilted into the outer border. The resulting open areas were quilted with large stars; and, as was common, the inner edge was finished with a scalloped quilting design.

B. Detail of outer corner block: A large wreath containing a star blends nicely with the rest of the border. A star motif also is used in the interior small corner block.

C. Although the format of the quilt and its central block are square, the pieced inner border has only three symmetrical corners. This may have been due to some fabric stretching or error in calculation or cutting that required the quilter to make some innovative adjustment. Such instances point out the fluid nature of the fabric medium and the expertise required in the art of quiltmaking.

D. Each of the central area open blocks is quilted with a circular petal design containing a central star. This is one of a wide variety of repetitive designs utilized by Amish quilters in their block quilts.

Plate 61

Ninepatch: Top: plain- and twill-weave cotton; back: green twill-print, plain-weave cotton; c. 1930. The quilt was purchased from a member of the Zook family in Lancaster County and thought to have been made about 1930.[10] The maker of this Ninepatch design created a quilt more within the usual parameters of Lancaster County quiltmaking than those previously illustrated. The traditional four corner blocks, the outside border feather quilting, and a framed center portion with the pieced block alternating with a plain block are all present.

Double Ninepatch

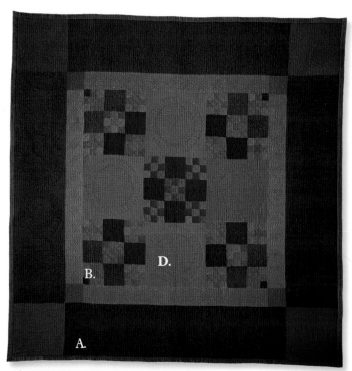

Outer dimensions: 79"
square
Binding: 1.25"
Outer border: 12"
Inner border: 4.25"
Center large open block:
14.625" square
Center small open block:
4.875" square
Individual small block:
1.625"

A. Detail of outer border: The robust and tightly curving feather quilting adds to the spectacular appearance of this quilt. Compare this example to the border quilting on the previous example (Plate 61).

C. Detail of back: The black-and-white backing is only one of the many variations of small geometric-woven cottons found on Lancaster County Amish quilts.

D. The fine quilting in the outer border continues in the large wreath design of the open center squares. The skills of the designer and quilter of this piece are obvious.

B. Details of small open block and small corner block: Even the small block motifs are adeptly quilted.

Plate 62
Double Ninepatch. Top: plain-weave, twill-weave, and henrietta wool; back: black-and-white geometric pattern-woven cotton; c. 1910. The dark wool fabrics and traditional quilting designs suggest an early 1900s date. The large scale of the Double Ninepatch center makes this quilt unusual.

Double Ninepatch

Overall dimensions: 82" square
Binding: 1.25"
Outer border: 12"
Inner border: 4"
Sashing: 2.375"
Small block: 1.125" square

A. Detail of turquoise sashing: The turquoise sashing carries the eye in from the outer area turquoise corner blocks. Here in the sashing the maker has quilted rows of hearts intersecting at corners with a star. This is an interesting variation to an otherwise traditional quilting pattern.

Plate 64
Double Ninepatch. Top: plain- and twill-weave wool; back: black-and-white woven-stripe plain-weave cotton; c. 1925. This example is the most complex of the Ninepatch variations set on square. They are less common than the Ninepatch and Double Ninepatch quilts set on point as seen in Plates 65 through 71.

Ninepatch

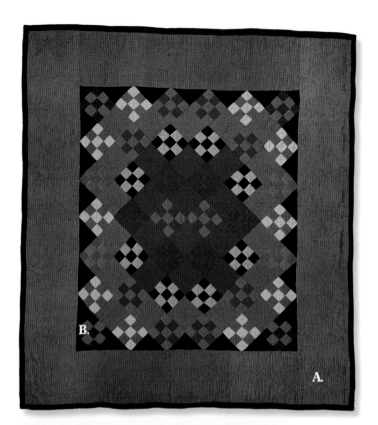

Overall dimensions: 75" x 84"
Binding: 1.25"
Outer border: 12"
Small block: 2" square

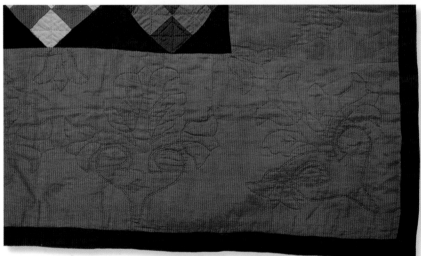

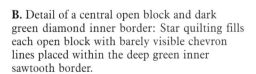

A. Detail of outer border: The heart and tulip motif is an uncommon but pleasing design. Note the individual tulip arising from each of the four corners.

B. Detail of a central open block and dark green diamond inner border: Star quilting fills each open block with barely visible chevron lines placed within the deep green inner sawtooth border.

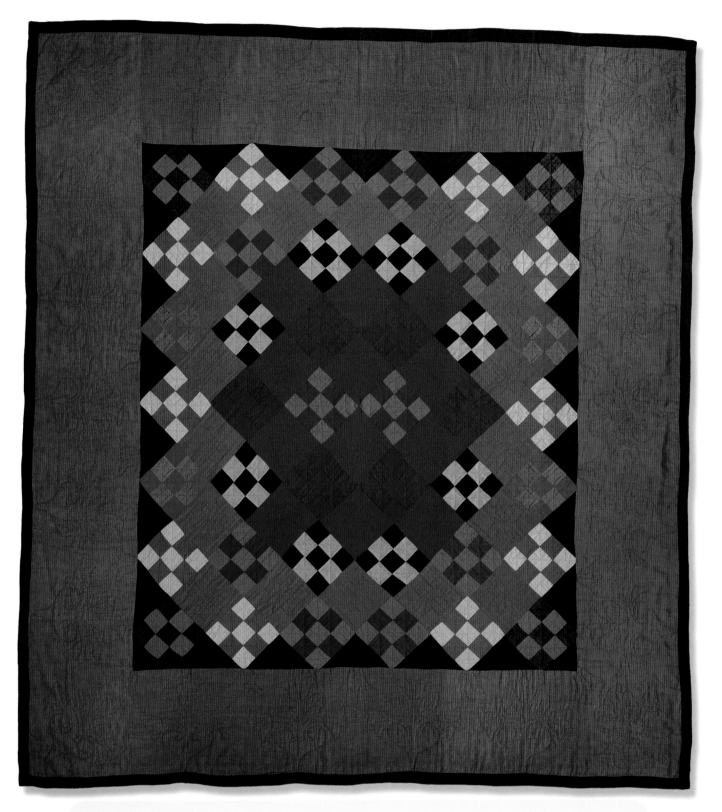

Plate 65

Ninepatch. Top: plain- and twill-weave wool, rayon, and cotton; back: black-and-white cotton chambray; c. 1935. The Ninepatch pattern and its variations were made by the Lancaster County Amish, but not, relatively speaking, in the proportion in which they are represented in this collection. Starting with this example the following block designs are "set on point." The maker has managed this successfully and manipulated colors to create visual excitement and a central focal point.

Overall dimensions: 89" square
Binding: 1"
Outer border: 9"
Sashing: 3"
Small block: 3" square

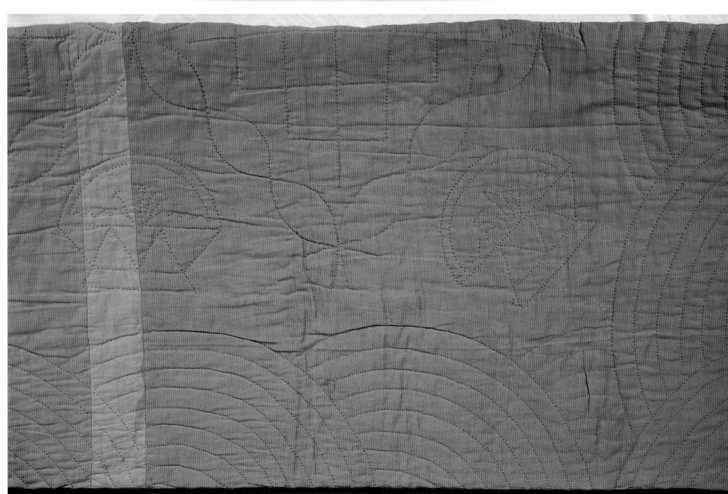

A. Detail of large dark triangles, photo from back: Better seen from the brown sateen cotton back, unusual basket motifs have been inserted in each of the black triangular border areas.

B. The fan quilting pattern found here may also be seen in the quilts pictured in Plates 55 and 56, two other relatively early examples in the collection.

Plate 66

Ninepatch. Top: plain- and twill-weave wool; back: brown sateen cotton; c. 1900. This quilt was made for Mary Blank of Monterey, a small settlement in eastern Lancaster County.[11] As with many early examples, the quilting is quite individualized in this piece.

Double Ninepatch

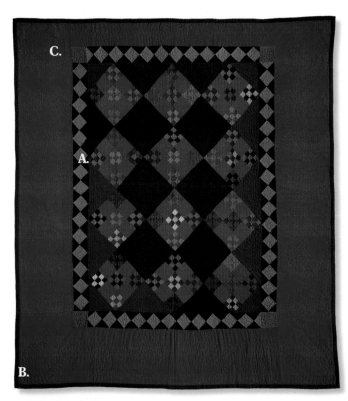

Overall dimensions: 77 x 85"
Binding: 1"
Outer border-side and bottom: 12.5"
Top border: 5.5"
Inner border: 3.75
Small block: 1" square

A. Detail of open center half-block: The quilter chose half- and quarter wreaths, along with full wreaths, to fill the open center blocks. The wreath is one of the most commonly used motifs for this purpose. The maker used two similar, but not matching, purple materials for the triangular blocks.

B. Detail of back with initials: The usual method of labeling an Amish quilt seems to have been to put the owner's or maker's initials in cross-stitch on the back of the quilt near the border. Here they were cross-stitched with light green cotton thread. The binding appears to have been replaced by hand at some time. Machine stitching from the original binding still remains.

C. Notice how the quilter has adjusted the feather design used in the three wide outer border areas to fit within the narrow top border.

Plate 67

Double Ninepatch. Top: plain-weave, twill-weave, and crepe wool; back: black-and-green printed cotton; c. 1919. This quilt, which bears the initials "A E," was made for Annie Esh before her marriage in 1919 to John Stoltzfus.[12] The top outer border of the quilt is narrower than the other three borders, suggesting that this end would be placed at the head of the bed. The introduction of a contrasting-color diamond-pieced inner border adds interest to an already busy pattern. *Gift of Irene N. Walsh.*

Double Ninepatch

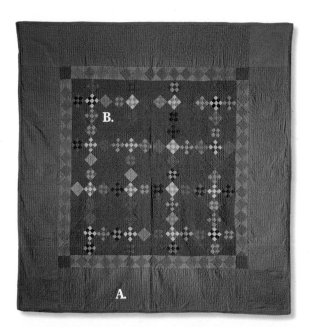

Overall dimensions: 85" square
Binding: 1.25"
Outer border: 12"
Inner border: 3.75"
Small block: 1" square

A. Detail of middle of outer border: The open space between the two curling feathers is filled in with two multi-petal flowers, just as was done in the previous quilt.

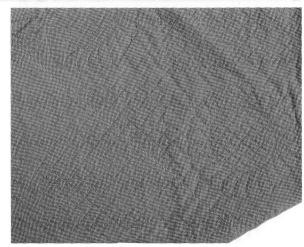

B. Detail of open block from back: A feather wreath similar to that of the previous example was also used in the open blocks. Here it is seen from the back of the quilt, better showing the quilting pattern and the polka-dot cotton backing material.

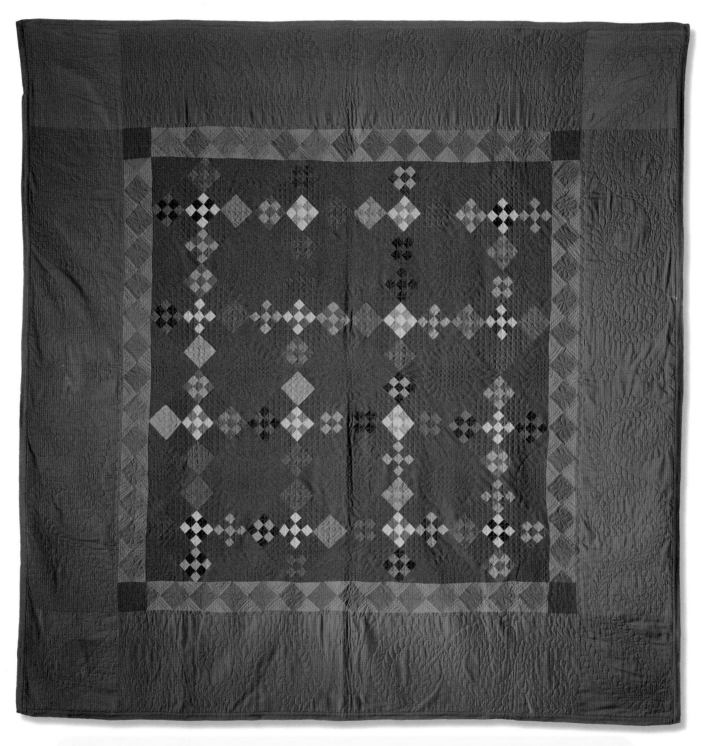

Plate 68

Double Ninepatch. Top: plain-weave crepe and henrietta wool; back: black-and-white polka-dot print plain-weave cotton; c. 1930. There are many similarities of salient features in this and the previous quilt (Plate 67). Here the maker has chosen to emphasize the center block of the large Ninepatch blocks with contrasting light pink squares. The effect livens the dark color scheme. Because of the similarities in pattern scale and quilting, it is possible that the same maker or group of makers produced these two quilts.

Double Ninepatch

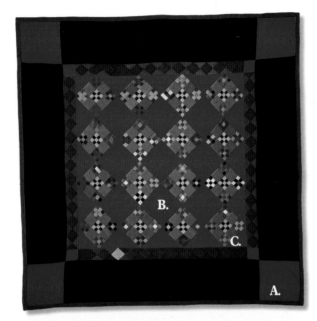

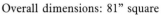

Overall dimensions: 81" square
Binding: 1.5"
Outer border: 11.5"
Inner border: 3.5
Small block: .875" square

B. Detail of open block in central area: Dorothy chose to fill her open blocks with stars and half stars.

A. Detail of corner block: The lovely feather quilting adds interest and dimension to the bright red corner blocks.

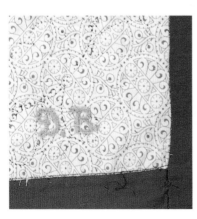

D. Detail of back: The maker's initials, "DB," appear where expected, cross-stitched near the back edge of a corner of the quilt. This cotton backing is probably one of the largest scale printed fabrics to be found on a Lancaster County Amish quilt.

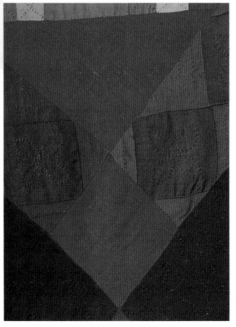

C. Detail of inner corner block and triangle at corner of center block: The finishing touch was added by quilting a small star in the corner triangles and a simple heart in each of the inner corner blocks.

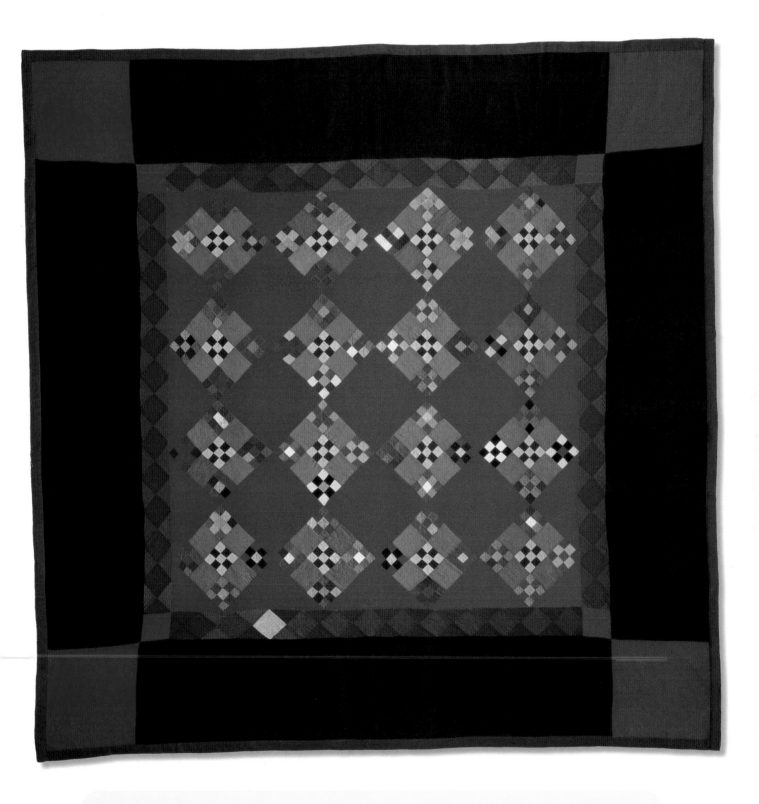

Plate 69

Double Ninepatch. Top: plain-weave, twill-weave, and crepe wool and rayon; back: blue-and-white printed plain-weave cotton; c. 1929. Attributed to Dorothy Beiler.[13] One wonders why the maker chose to put one light patch in her diamond inner border, but this certainly does not take away from the stunning effect of her quilt. *Gift in memory of Emily Kauffman Hartman Delp and Robert Eugene Delp.*

Double Ninepatch

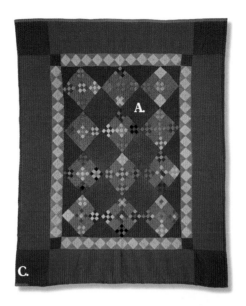

Overall dimensions: 67" x 81"
Binding: 1"
Outer border: 9.5"
Inner border: 3.5
Small block: 1" square

A. Detail of open center block: An intricate interlacing circular device has been quilted within the purple open squares. A technique, not usually seen in Lancaster County Amish quilts, was used when piecing this central area. Each open purple block was top-stitched in place. This could indicate that the open purple blocks were replaced at some later date. Notice that each block is machine-stitched with black thread through the full thickness of the quilt. This can be appreciated better from the back of the quilt.

B. Detail of back: The machine stitching around each large central block shows well on the plain red backing.

C. Detail of back with initials: The initials "RE," cross-stitched with light tan cotton thread, are found as might be expected, near the edge of the back. This may identify the maker or the owner.

Plate 70

Double Ninepatch. Top: plain- and twill-weave wool; back: red plain-weave cotton; c. 1925. Compared to the previous quilt (Plate 69) a lighter palate of fabrics appears in this example. The prominent yellow diamonds within the inner border are a departure from the usual Amish colors. This quilt is signed on the back with the initials "RE."

Double Ninepatch

Overall dimensions: 85" square
Binding: 1.5"
Outer border: 12"
Inner border: 4"
Small block: 1" square

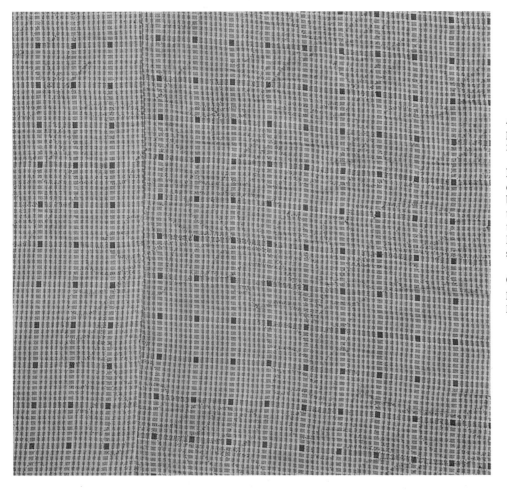

A. Detail of back: A handsome printed cotton material adds the finishing touch to this fine quilt.

B. Exceptionally robust feather quilting is used in the border. The branches curve into tight circles and the open areas are supplemented with triangular clamshell quilting that also lines the inner borders to form a scalloped edge.

C. The open blocks are quilted in a pattern similar to the one used in the previous example.

Plate 71
Double Ninepatch. Top: plain- and twill-weave wool; back: tan-and-brown plaid-print, plain-weave cotton; c. 1930. A wide variety of well-distributed blocks of color and exquisite quilting combine to produce a spectacular bedcovering. *Gift of Anne L. and Robert K. Bowman Family Foundation.*

Courthouse Square

Overall dimensions: 77" square
Binding: 1"
Outer border: 10.25"
Inner large block: 8.25"
Small block: 1.25" square

A. Detail of outer border and corner from back: Lovely basket quilting is complemented by the well-designed floral motif that fits well into each corner. The quilting patterns show best against the gold background of the cotton back.

B. Detail of center open block from back: The wreath quilting in the open center blocks is also better seen through the lighter backing fabric.

Plate 72

Courthouse Square. Top: twill-weave and henrietta wool; back: gold plain-weave cotton; c. 1920. The Courthouse Square arrangement of blocks is an unusual design to be found in a Lancaster County Amish quilt, but the traditional quilting patterns are what one would expect. The outer gray-blue triangular blocks bordering the central portion of the quilt set off this section of an otherwise dark quilt. They are quilted in a chevron design. Like some of the other rarely occurring patterns in this collection, it is likely that the Amish maker was influenced by neighboring "English" quilters.

Basket of Chips

Overall dimensions: 74" x 76"
Binding: 0.5"
Outer border: 11.25"
Inner border: 4"
Sashing: 2.75"
Inner large block: 7.75"

A. Detail of binding from back. The binding is unusually narrow, measuring only 0.5 inch. It is made from a twill wool material and is hand-finished.

B. The segments of the feather design almost touch in some areas. In other areas there is more open space at the juncture.

C. The presence of sashing in a Basket pattern and the clamshell quilting within it sets this piece apart from the usual Lancaster County Amish block quilt.

Plate 73

Basket of Chips. Top: plain- and twill-weave wool; back: tan plain-weave cotton; c. 1925. Basket-pattern quilts were made by a small group of Amish women in Lancaster County, but the usual form is similar to the next example, seen in Plate 74. This Basket of Chips, with sashing separating the motifs, was rarely used by the Lancaster community.

Baskets

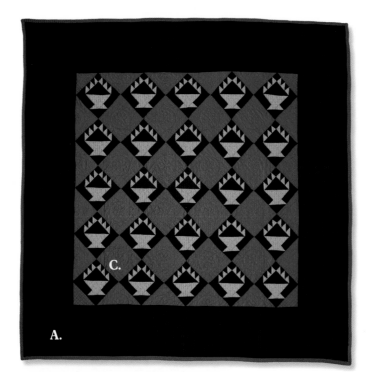

Overall dimensions: 82.5" square
Binding: 1"
Outer border: 12.25"
Inner block: 8"

A. Detail of outer border: The intertwining floral designs tied off with bows in each corner are almost identical to an example, in the Heritage Center Museum's collection, made by Sarah Stoltzfus for her brother Samuel around 1939. She also made similar quilts for herself and for each of her three other siblings.

B. Detail of back: Two handsome crisp cotton materials have been used in the backing. The floral material is a print and the plaid is a woven pattern.

C. The circular motif in the open block is similar to the variations used in the other related Baskets quilts.

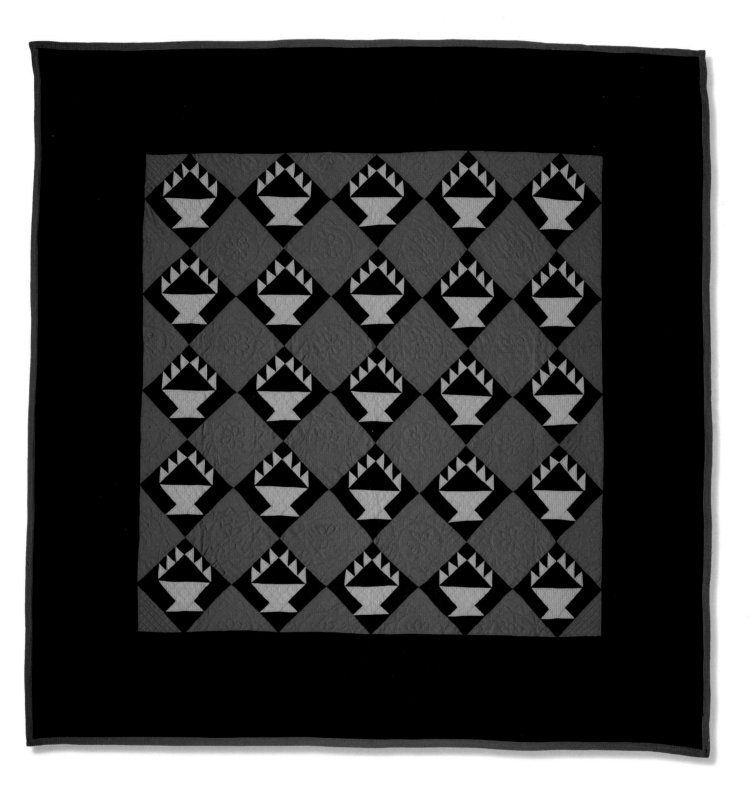

Plate 74
Baskets. Top: plain-weave and crepe wool; back: black-and-white floral print and blue-and-white woven-plaid, plain-weave cotton; c. 1935. Attributed to makers in the Lapp, Stoltzfus, or Glick families, Salisbury Township. Fewer than ten of these Basket quilts are known and they seem to have been made by and for members of these neighboring and related families.[14]

Crazy Quilt

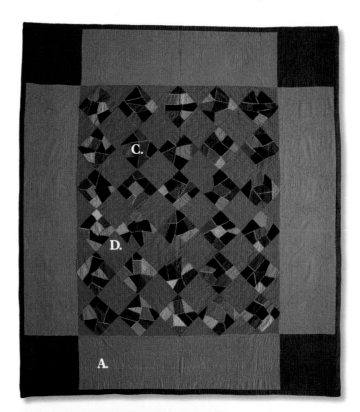

Overall dimensions: 71" x 79"
Binding: 1.25"
Outer border: 12."
Inner block: 6.5"

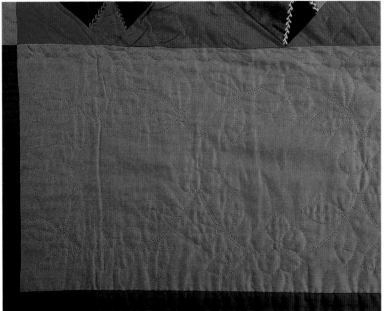

A. Detail of border: The floral wreath border quilting is a pattern seen frequently in mid- 1930s quilts.

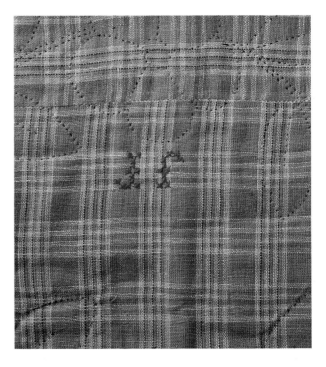

B. Detail of initials on back: This rather bright-colored plaid backing fabric is indicative of the later dating of this quilt. Here the maker's or owner's initials have been cross-stitched with red cotton thread.

C. Seldom is surface needlework used in Lancaster County Amish quilts. The few known Fan and Crazy Quilts are the most notable exceptions.

D. The six-pointed star with double-outline quilting nicely complements the busier adjacent Crazy patches.

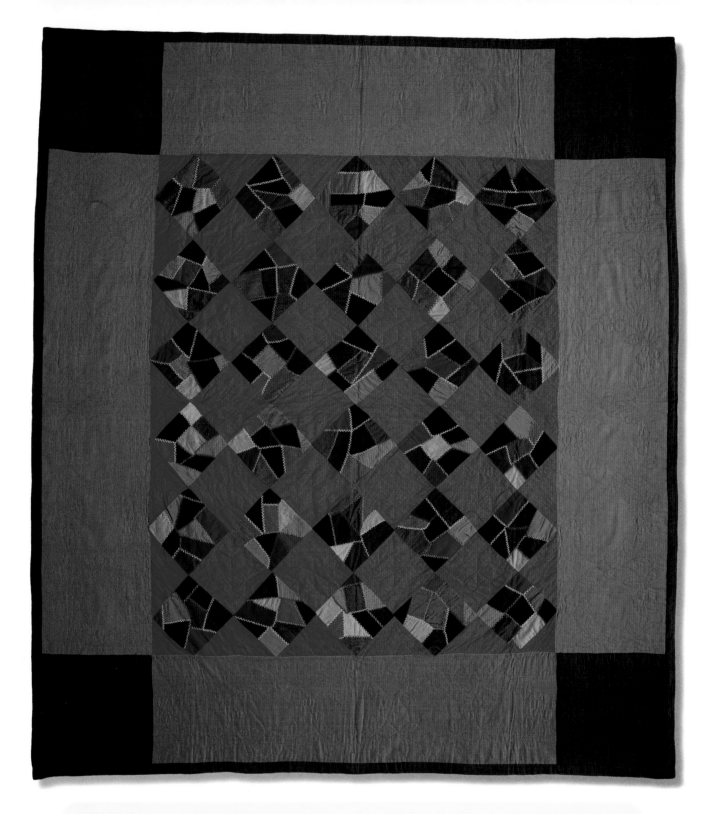

Plate 75

Crazy Quilt: Top: plain-weave, twill-weave and crepe wool and cotton decorated with cotton embroidery floss; back: purple, black, and yellow woven-plaid, plain-weave cotton; c. 1933. A small group of closely related Crazy Quilts was made by members of the Lancaster County Amish community. All but one, shown in Plate 78, are constructed with alternating Crazy blocks on point set off by plain blocks. Several of this pattern are dated (see Plates 76 and 78) and occasionally initialed within the top pattern. This example is initialed "JF" on the back. Never as wild and freely constructed as neighboring "English" Crazy Quilts, these reserved Amish renditions were made long after the late-nineteenth-century Crazy Quilt rage had subsided in other quilting populations. One might describe the Amish form as a controlled Crazy Quilt! *Gift of Irene N. Walsh.*

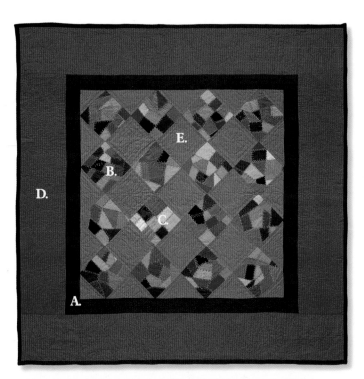

Overall dimensions: 80" square
Binding: 1"
Outer border: 10.75"
Inner border: 3.5"
Inner block: 8.75"

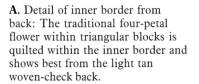

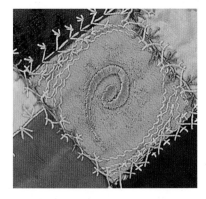

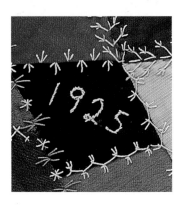

A. Detail of inner border from back: The traditional four-petal flower within triangular blocks is quilted within the inner border and shows best from the light tan woven-check back.

C. Detail of square with silver embroidered material: The maker of this quilt has included two pieces of fanciful commercial needlework-decorated silver material in her quilt. This is not a fabric that would have been used in any other place in an Amish home.

D. Well-executed quilting designs appear throughout the quilt and are reminiscent of the type and quality seen in earlier quilts in the collection. Here the feathers have a tight curl and the eight-petal flowers fill the open areas.

B. Detail of dated block: The date of 1925 has been added to the black square with simple cotton-floss outline stitch. Note the variety of embroidery stitches that embellish the Crazy blocks.

E. The flower fill-in motifs are reflected again in the center open blocks. Even more area is filled in with scalloped borders along the edge of each block.

Plate 76

Crazy Quilt: Top: plain-weave, pattern-weave, and crepe wool, twill-weave wool, and rayon blend, cotton embroidery floss; back: tan woven-check cotton; 1925. This is an important quilt, because it is possibly the earliest dated example of this small group of Lancaster County, Pennsylvania Crazy Quilts. *Gift of Irene N. Walsh.*

Crazy Quilt

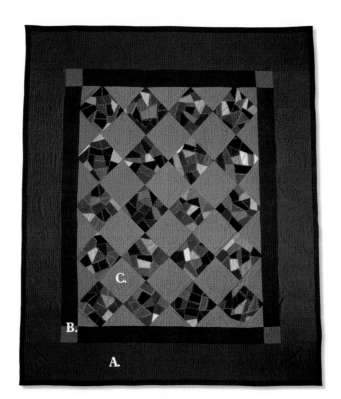

Overall dimensions: 79" x 92"
Binding: 1.5"
Outer border: 9.5"
Inner border: 4.25"
Inner block: 9"

A. Detail of outer border: The classic feather quilting fills an outer border that is proportionally more narrow than is found in the previous example. In this case there was no room or need to fill open areas with additional quilting motifs.

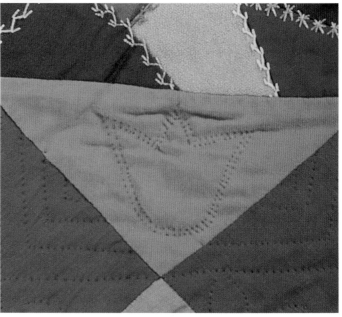

B. Detail of corner triangle in center area: Notice the departure from traditionally quartering the wreath motif for the small corner block. Instead, the maker has chosen to place a small tulip in each corner triangle.

C. Another classic quilting motif, the wreath, was chosen to fill the open center blocks.

Plate 77

Crazy Quilt: Top: plain-weave, twill-weave, and crepe wool, cotton embroidery floss; back: black-and-white woven-check, plain-weave cotton; c. 1925. This undated quilt is another fine example of the Crazy Quilt pattern. There are four similar pieces in the collection, but one cannot assume it was a common pattern among the Lancaster County Amish. As with the Baskets pattern, they consist of a small group of similar quilts, influenced by the local "English" traditions, and likely made by a closely related group of Amish women. This example is noticeably rectangular.

Crazy Quilt

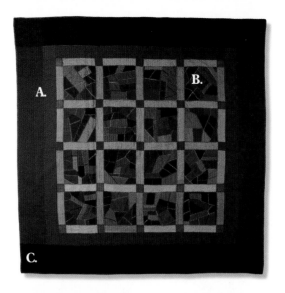

Overall dimensions:
81"square
Outer border: 9.25"
Inner border: 4"
Inner block: 10.5"
Sashing: 2.5"

A. Detail of outer and inner borders and sashing: The light green quilting thread was chosen for use against the dark green wool border. Using a contrasting-color quilting thread became a more common practice in Lancaster County Amish quilts made in the mid-twentieth century. In this piece it is used throughout the quilt. The quilting patterns also reflect the later time period in which the quilt was made.

C. Detail of edge: The initials "CS" were chain-stitched along the back edge. This is the only quilt in the collection that does not have an applied wide binding. The maker chose to turn the front edge to the back and hand-stitch it into place. Although this is a common technique used by other quilters, it is rare to find this in a Lancaster County Amish quilt.

B. Detail of dated block: It is not common practice to quilt Crazy patches, so the embellishment here is done with a wild variety of colored cotton embroidery floss and a fluorescent pink two-tone chain-stitched date.

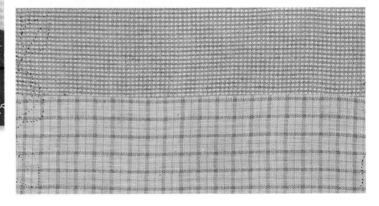

D. Detail of back: The back of the quilt is made up of two interesting woven-patterned pieces of cotton yardage.

Plate 78
Crazy Quilt: Top: plain-weave, twill-weave, and crepe wool, cotton embroidery floss; back: multicolor woven-plaid and check, plain-weave cotton; 1938. This dated quilt, probably one of the most recently made quilts in the collection, is also signed "CS." Other unusual aspects are the lack of an applied binding, blocks placed on a square, the absence of open blocks in the central area, and the use of contrasting quilting thread.

Sawtooth Diamond

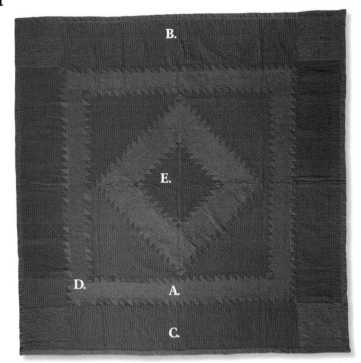

Overall dimensions: 81.5" square
Binding: 1.5"
Outer border: 10.5"
Inner border: 3.75"
Central diamond border: 6"
Large inner square: 43"
Inner diamond: 12.5"
Sawtooth block: 1.75

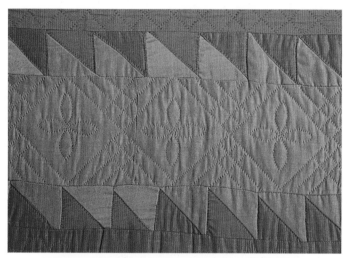

B. Detail of initials on outer border: The initials and date are quilted into the middle of the two outer wide opposite borders.

A. Detail of inner sawtooth border: The quilter has chosen to alter the feather quilting to suitably fit this inner wide border.

C. Detail of date: 1925 probably notes the year in which this quilt was made.

D. Notice the adroit manner in which the maker resolved the dilemma of how to handle the Sawtooth sections at the corners. The traditional Amish quilting patterns also adapt well to the wider sawtooth border. Stars are used as corner accents.

E. The finely quilted wreath and central multi-petal flower perfectly finish this superb example of a quilt.

Plate 79

Sawtooth Diamond: Top: plain-weave wool; back: blue-and-white cotton chambray; 1925. Although one could classify this pattern as a Center Diamond variation it was not a pattern commonly used by the Lancaster County Amish. Mennonite neighbors frequently created Sawtooth Diamond quilts, often in similar contrasting solid colors, but they used cotton fabrics and not the fine wools seen in this example. Fortunately, the owner or maker identified this piece with the quilted initials and date "SZ" and "1925." *Gift of Lancaster County Foundation.*

Double Irish Chain

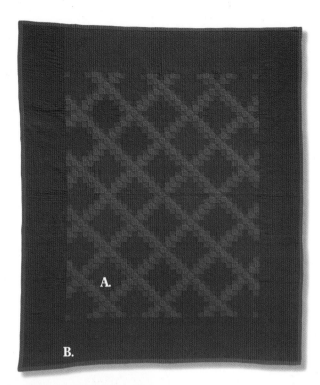

Overall dimensions: 70.5" x 84"
Binding: 1"
Outer border: 10.25"
Block: 1.375"

A. Detail of central open block and surrounding blue squares: The star quilting pattern also was used to fill the open areas in Amish block-patterned quilts. Note how the maker applied each of the blue blocks onto the purple ground with machine stitching.

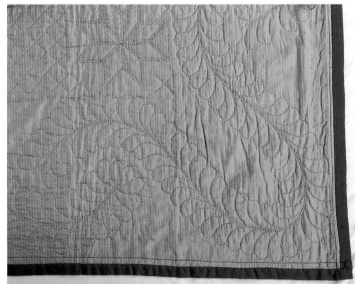

B. Detail of outer border from back: The classic feather quilting executed with dark-colored cotton thread on a dark purple outer border is better seen from the light green back.

Plate 80

Double Irish Chain: Top: plain- and twill-weave wool, back: light-green twill-weave cotton; c. 1920.
Fine classic Lancaster County Amish quilting has been applied to a non-traditional Irish Chain pattern.
Although there are two examples in the collection, the pattern was much more frequently used by the
Amish families' Mennonite neighbors. Mennonite quilts were of cotton and frequently used small-scale
printed fabrics.

Triple Irish Chain

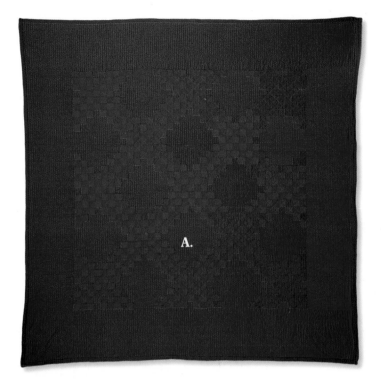

A.

Overall dimensions: 81" square
Binding: 1.25"
Outer border: 11"
Block: 1.625"

A. Detail of center open block showing surrounding row of squares: In this Irish Chain quilt the maker chose to apply the blue blocks onto the red open areas by hand.

B. Detail of back: Would one expect to see such a busy printed cotton backing applied to this bold deep-colored top? Here it works beautifully!

Plate 81
Triple Irish Chain: Top: plain-weave wool; back: blue, black, and white floral-print, plain-weave cotton; c. 1925. This vibrant red, blue, and green combination is a superb example of why Lancaster County Amish quilts appeal to the art quilt collector. Enhanced by the sculptural quilting, the piece is a pleasure to behold. *Gift of Irene N. Walsh.*

Lone Star

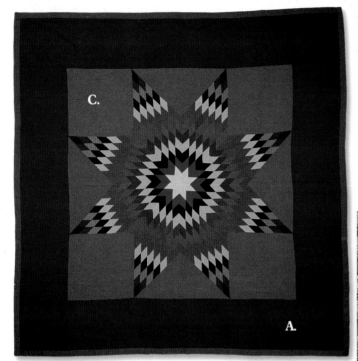

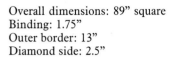

Overall dimensions: 89" square
Binding: 1.75"
Outer border: 13"
Diamond side: 2.5"

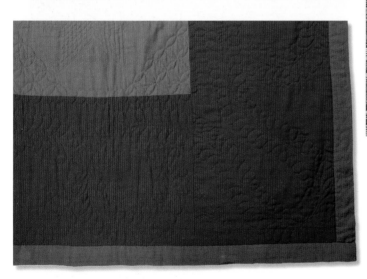

A. Detail of outer border: The feather quilting with added scallop edging on the inner border perfectly complements the simple setting around the central motif.

B. Detail of back: The backing material is almost as much of a surprise as the spectacular top. This bright three-color plaid print does not disappoint the curious who care to turn back a corner.

C. Instead of filling the whole field with fine waffle quilting the maker chose to embellish each corner with a finely quilted star surrounded by intersecting small circles.

(Endnotes)
[1] Robert Hughes, *Amish the Art of the Quilt* (New York: Alfred A. Knopf, 1990), facing Plate 4.
[2] Ibid., facing Plate 12.
[3] Ibid., facing Plate 25.
[4] Ibid., facing Plate 26.
[5] Ibid., facing Plate 27.
[6] Ibid., facing Plate 34.
[7] Ibid., facing Plate 41.
[8] Ibid., facing Plate 42
[9] Daniel and Kathryn McCauley, *Decorative Arts of the Amish of Lancaster County* (Intercourse, Pa.: Good Books, 1988), p. 60.
[10] Hughes, *Amish the Art of the Quilt*, facing Plate 59.
[11] Ibid., facing Plate 65.
[12] Ibid., facing Plate 67.
[13] Ibid., facing Plate 69.
[14] Patricia T. Herr, *Amish Arts of Lancaster County* (Atglen, Pa.: Schiffer Publishing Ltd., 1998), pp. 86-88, and Patricia T. Herr *Quilting Traditions: Pieces from the Past* (Atglen, Pa. : Schiffer Publishing Ltd., 2000), pp 58-62.

Plate 82

Lone Star: Top: plain-weave wool; back: red, green, and white printed-plaid, plain-weave cotton; c. 1920. What a perfect quilt to show as the final piece in this exquisite collection of stars of the Lancaster County Amish quilt world! The Lone Star is a rare form and this is among the finest of its type. The impact of the single motif pattern is enhanced by the surprise appearance of yellow in the center of the star. Yellow is not a color commonly found in Lancaster County Amish quilts, and here it adds to the varied triangular color bands so expertly pieced into a star. *Gift of Irene N. Walsh.*

Glossary

A few terms are mentioned here to help the reader with some of the more common fabric and textile names used in the description of Amish quilts.[1]

BATISTE: Derived from the name of a well-known French linen weaver, Jean Batiste, the fabric is a fine plain-weave material that can be made from a variety of fibers—cotton, wool, and synthetics. As it is used in the world of Lancaster County Amish quilts, it denotes sheer high-quality wool, frequently used as a dress material and in quilt tops.

CHALLIS: This lightweight fabric is known for its draping qualities of a tighter weave than batiste. It may be a plain- or twill-weave fabric woven from a variety and combination of fibers, natural and synthetic. The Amish of Lancaster used it extensively for dress and quilt-top material.

CHAMBRAY: Made from cotton, rayon, or polyester, chambray is a plain-weave fabric used by the Lancaster County Amish in clothing and extensively as quilt backing. It has a lustrous or frosted appearance, created by weaving with a colored fiber as warp and a white fiber as the weft or filler.

CREPE: This denotes a fabric woven from highly spun or over-twisted yarns that may have been specially treated to result in a pebbly or puckered surface. Originally used as a term in silk weaving, in Lancaster Amish quilts crepe describes wool or rayon yarns that appeared in quilt made in the late 1930s and the 1940s.

HENRIETTA CLOTH: The original henrietta cloth, used in late nineteenth and early twentieth century Lancaster quilts, was woven using a silk warp and a woolen weft. In most cases the fibers were of two different colors, giving a special sheen to the fabric that was particularly favored by the Amish. The term also was used for plain-weave woolens with a glossy finish. The fabric became unavailable by the 1920s and therefore is associated only with earlier quilts.

MERCERIZING: A process of finishing yarns named after John Mercer who developed the technique in 1850. Yarns, usually cotton, are impregnated with cold concentrated sodium hydroxide solution creating a fiber with more luster, dyeability and stretch.

PLAIN WEAVE: This is the simplest of weave patterns, often referred to by weavers as tabby. It comprises two fibers similar in weight and spacing. The fiber or yarn running lengthwise in the cloth is called the **WARP**. The fiber running crosswise is referred to as the **WEFT**, **FILLER**, or **WOOF**. In its simplest form the two yarns interlace by going alternately under and over each other at each intersection. In Lancaster County quilts plain-weave fabrics of natural and artificial materials are used on both the front and the back of the quilt.

RAYON: A synthetic material, rayon was first developed using cellulose products in Europe in the nineteenth century. It was widely marketed in the United States after 1910 as a substitute for silk in hosiery and other knitted products. By the mid 1920s it began to replace most natural fabrics so that by the 1940s the wools normally used by the Amish for clothing and quilt tops had been supplanted almost entirely by rayon products.

SATEEN: This term may be used in a variety of ways, either as a weave structure or as the appearance of a fabric. The satin (or sateen) weave structure has long floats, or lengths of warp or weft fibers running over the top of the cloth, producing a sheen.[2] Some twill-weave structures produce the same effect. Also, plain-weave fabrics made from mercerized or otherwise processed yarns produce a sheen that is similar. Within the context of Amish quilt-making, it is usually understood to mean any cotton or rayon cloth that has a shiny or lustrous surface. Sateen fabrics became popular in the 1920s.

TWILL WEAVE: This weave is characterized by diagonal lines in the fabric. A minimum of three warp groupings is necessary, with each of those yarns traveling repetitively in a separate path one step from its neighbor. These steps produce a shift to the left or the right, resulting in continuous diagonal lines showing on each side of the fabric.

[1] Definitions listed here have been drawn from a more complete glossary found in Eve Wheatcroft Granick, *The Amish Quilt* (Intercourse, Pa.: Good Books, 1989), 180-86.

[2] For a detailed analysis of sateen and other weave structures see Irene Emery, *The Primary Structures of Fabrics* (Washington, D.C.: The Textile Museum, 1980).

Bibliography

Beiler, Katie, ed. *Descendants and History of Christian Fisher (1757-1838), Third Edition.* Lancaster, Pa.: Eby's Quality Printing, 1988.

Bishop, Robert, and Elizabeth Safanda. *A Gallery of Amish Quilts: Design Diversity from a Plain People.* New York: E. P. Dutton & Co., Inc., 1976.

Burnham, Dorothy K. *Warp and Weft: A Textile Terminology.* Toronto: Royal Ontario Museum, 1980.

Emery, Irene. *The Primary Structures of Fabrics: an Illustrated Classification.* Washington: The Textile Museum, Washington, D.C., 1980.

Gingerich, Hugh F., and Rachel W. Kreider. *Amish and Amish Mennonite Genealogies.* Gordonville, Pa.: Pequea Publishers, 1986.

Granick, Eve Wheatcroft. *The Amish Quilt.* Intercourse, Pa.: Good Books, 1989

Herr, Patricia T. *Amish Arts of Lancaster County.* Atglen, Pa.: Schiffer Publishing Ltd., 1998.

____. *Quilting Traditions: Pieces from the Past.* Atglen, Pa.: Schiffer Publishing Ltd., 2000.

Hostetler, John A. *Amish Society.* 3d. ed. Baltimore: Johns Hopkins University Press, 1980.

____. *Amish Life.* Scottdale, Pa. and Kitchener, Ontario: Herald Press, 1983.

____ ed. *Amish Roots: A Treasury of History, Wisdom, and Lore.* Baltimore: Johns Hopkins University Press, 1989.

Kraybill, Donald B, and Marc A. Olshan. *The Amish Struggle with Modernity.* Hanover, New Hampshire: University Press of New England, 1994.

Holstein, Jonathan. *The Pieced Quilt.* Greenwich, Connecticut: New York Graphic Society Ltd., 1973.

Hughes, Robert, and Julie Silber. *Amish: The Art of the Quilt.* New York: Alfred A Knopf, 1990.

Keyser, Alan G. "Beds, Bedding, Bedsteads and Sleep." *Der Reggeboge (The Rainbow) Quarterly of the Pennsylvania German Society.* 12, no. 4 (October 1978): 1-28.

Kraybill, Donald B. *The Riddle of Amish Culture*, Rev. ed. Baltimore: Johns Hopkins University Press, 2001.

____. *The Amish and the State.* Baltimore: Johns Hopkins University Press, 2003.

Kraybill, Donald B., Patricia T. Herr, and Jonathan Holstein. *A Quiet Spirit: Amish Quilts from the Collection of Cindy Tietze and Stuart Hodash.* Los Angeles: UCLA Fowler Museum of Cultural History, 1996.

Lasansky, Jeannette, ed. *A Good Start: The Aussteier or Dowry.* Lewisburg, Pa.: Oral Traditions Project of Union County Historical Society, 1990.

Lestz, Gerald S., John W. W. Loose, and Benjamin Rush. *Amish: Culture and Economy.* Ephrata, Pa.: Science Press, 1984.

MacCauley, Daniel and Kathryn. *Decorative Arts of the Amish of Lancaster County.* Intercourse, Pa.: Good Books, 1988.

Pellman, Rachel and Kenneth. *Amish Crib Quilts.* Intercourse, Pa.: Good Books, 1985.

____. *A Treasury of Amish Quilts.* Intercourse, Pa.: Good Books, 1990.

____. *A Treasury of Mennonite Quilts.* Intercourse, Pa.: Good Books, 1992.

Index